# THE GREAT AMERICAN HOUSE

## TRADITION FOR THE WAY WE LIVE NOW

RIZZOLI
NEW YORK

New York Paris London Milan

# THE GREAT AMERICAN HOUSE

## TRADITION FOR THE WAY WE LIVE NOW

### GIL SCHAFER III
#### WRITTEN WITH MARC KRISTAL

The marvel of a Home is not that it shelters and warms a man,
nor that he owns its walls. It comes from those layers of
sweetness which it gradually stores up in us.
May it form, deep in our hearts, that obscure range of mountains
from which springs the sources of our dreams.

—*Wind, Sand and Stars,* Antoine de Saint-Exupéry

# TABLE OF CONTENTS

# FOREWORD

Over the years of my career I have had the opportunity to work with many wonderful architects, and Gil Schafer is at the top of the list. Whether he is designing a new house or renovating an existing building, his instincts are always perfect. His new buildings are creative and exciting, and his renovations and additions to buildings are so perfectly designed that it is almost impossible to know what was added. Gil listens to his clients to understand their lifestyle and spends time exploring their vision for a home and how they want to live. He makes dreams come true.

Gil is a trained classical architect. His sense of proportion and scale is amazing. But what sets Gil apart from others is his flair for design. He understands how a house must flow so that his floor plans gracefully lead from one room to another while creating amazing vistas within a house. His attention to detail is unsurpassed and especially creative. Gil's houses feel as though they have always been there. His selection of honed, mellow stones, hand-scraped polished floors, patinated hardware, and rich French-polished doors always makes it hard to believe that this is a new house. Each room is given its own attention to detail and character, creating a sense of surprise as you move through the house. Gil also thinks like an interior designer; as he designs, he is aware of how furniture can be placed in a room to make it comfortable. He never builds awkward rooms that are impossible to furnish.

A Gil Schafer house is not only beautiful but also practical. He understands how important the service parts of a house are. There are always plenty of closets and pantries, an ample mudroom, functional laundry rooms, and luxurious bathrooms. Everything that is needed to make a house function is carefully considered and planned.

Not only does Gil understand how a house must flow, but he also has an amazing sense of siting a house on a piece of property. He thinks like a landscape designer, developing a site plan as a part of the whole process. He creates exciting entrances and provides doors and windows that connect the inside to the outside. Terraces and porches are all planned with respect to the building site and light; views are created from each opening. There is complete harmony between his houses and the landscape.

Gil is a very talented architect, but even more important, he is a dear friend. He is a man with a great sense of humor as well as a great sense of personal style—he is one of the best-dressed men I know. His own house and apartment are elegant, comfortable, and welcoming for his many friends. We have had wonderful trips shopping in France, often vying for the same things. He gives unselfishly to things he is passionate about. His commitment to architecture and design have led him to unselfishly commit thousands of hours to the development of the Institute of Classical Architecture & Art, an institution devoted to the advanced study of traditional architecture. It was his dedication that helped nurture and grow this amazing organization. Gil is a renaissance man, a person who is trained as a classicist but creates amazing homes for today's lifestyles.

—*Bunny Williams*

# INTRODUCTION

During my nearly twenty-five years as an architect of classical residences, I have worked on scores of projects—of different sizes, preexisting and from the ground up, in numerous locations, under conditions simple and complex, and for every sort of client. But I still find myself beginning every job the same way: by reaching back into my own memories of home and the places that have had meaning for me over the years, which to this day remain powerful touchstones and reference points. I have come to realize that it is these houses and landscapes from my past that give my work its particular character and, hopefully, its individuality.

I grew up living in a variety of regions around the country: the Midwest, where I was born and where much of my family is from; a farm on the East Coast, where I spent most of my childhood; New York City, where my dad lived; a grandparent's hunting plantation in Georgia; a beach house on the coast of California, and, later, one in the Bahamas. As a result, I found myself exposed to and intrigued by a wide array of building traditions and contexts. I also had a grandfather who was an architect and parents who were *always* constructing, renovating, or decorating something, so I was attuned to architecture—as well as decoration and landscape—from a very young age.

I think I was very lucky to have been exposed to so many interesting places growing up because they helped to define my sensibility and taste. Many of these were family houses, and from them I began to have an intuitive sense of the continuity of tradition as an essential characteristic of places that were called "home." My maternal grandmother's house is a perfect example. Every fall, she would leave a brick-and-half-timbered Norman-style house where she lived during the summers, in the countryside near Cleveland, Ohio, and return to southern Georgia, to a family property called Melrose Plantation; it had belonged to her father before her and to his father before that. Her house in the north was compact,

Growing up, I was drawn to Maxfield Parrish's evocative New England landscapes, like this one, *New Moon*, from 1958. The feelings these paintings elicited—with the setting sun on a facade, the lights welcoming one from within, and a delicate moon suspended above it all— somehow captured for me the intangible qualities of home.

dark, and had rooms that felt cut off from the outdoors, but Melrose was light, airy, and sprawling. It was also pink.

There was something utterly magical about this perfectly well-mannered, classical house that also happened to be pink. And the house suited my grandmother: like her, it was dignified and stylish but never flashy, never pompous. It was also an essay in elegant understatement and, as I look back on it now, one of the houses that has shaped my taste the most. Its entry portico and front door brought you into gracious rooms and introduced the promise of a beautiful garden on the other side of its center hall. That sense of anticipation and surprise—something that began when you entered the property and traveled down its long driveway—is an experience I have tried to incorporate in some way into each of my own projects. Remarkably, the interior of the house remained essentially unchanged over its many generations of family ownership. Its residents obviously recognized the importance of tradition and continuity—values that I too have

come to believe are inherent in the idea of home.

As a child, I *loved* coming to Melrose—it was such a world of its own, and it was always an adventure to be there; it's where I learned about farming, horseback riding, and fishing, and how to milk a cow. When my brother and I weren't on the mule-drawn hunting wagon in the woods of tall longleaf pines or hanging out around the house and its gardens, we would take our bikes and go exploring, riding on the plantation's many miles of roads and around the village of outbuildings that made up the service core of the property. It was where I first began to understand that buildings can create a sense of place when they're grouped together artfully, and landscape can shape space and create views. Melrose taught me the relationship between a house and its gardens as well as the importance of the balance between the formality of a landscape around a house, and the informality of the wild landscape that might be its larger context. There I began to understand how that relationship contributes to the overall

experience of a place. That balance between the wild and the refined is one of the thrills of a large property like Melrose, and the interaction of those two kinds of landscape experiences is what made being there so unique and such a pleasure.

The house also taught me about charm and the important role it plays in making a grand property feel human and warm. At Melrose, there were all sorts of examples of charm at work: the old horseshoe over the front door, placed there for good luck; an intriguing doorknob with a carved face of a man on it; a beat-up bronze bucket, overflowing with cut branches, hung on the wall of a porch; an old leather satchel with the name *Melrose* stamped on its side, filled daily with the household mail. And, of course, the pink color was an essay in charm all by itself. I learned that it was the quirky things that make a house feel lived in and that architecture could create that feeling as powerfully as the objects that we put into our homes.

Inspired by these experiences—as well as by a love of architecture and its history—I decided to follow in my grandfather's footsteps and enroll as a graduate student in architecture at Yale. But once there, it became clear to me that these lessons from childhood weren't as valued in the academy. There, the principles of modernism and expressing, architecturally, the spirit of the modern age were at odds with a reverence for tradition and the aesthetic pursuit of something that was "charming."

After graduation, with my modernist credentials in hand and the beginnings of a career in pursuit of the avant-garde underway, I began to realize that I had lost touch with the things that had drawn me to architecture originally. In truth, I was much more interested in making places that spoke to my own memories and experiences, places with a more explicit connection to architectural history, than in the abstract theories of design championed by my formal education.

Feeling this disconnection from tradition ultimately led me to work in firms that practiced classical residential architecture and to get involved with the Institute of Classical Architecture in New York—a path, I came to believe, that would lead me to produce better work, or at least work that had more meaning to me. Together these experiences gave me my second education, and put me back in sync with what I loved in architecture and design on a visceral level—one that set me on a course focused on creating places for people to live and enjoy life that are comfortable and *also* have a feeling of history and memory. Once I made that transition, memories of my own life at Melrose and other family houses—and the architectural lessons I learned from them—became tremendously relevant again.

How do these lessons play out in practice? At the most basic level, I love resolving architectural problems and doing

so with design rooted in the restrained, understated classicism I knew growing up. I am also inspired by the quality and craftsmanship of those houses, and over the years I have pursued collaborations with extraordinary artisans, people who make the special things for the firm's projects that enliven and enrich our work.

The houses I knew growing up also taught me to be equally passionate about the fundamental roles that interior decoration and landscape play in the successful design of a great house. In terms of decoration, I think carefully about the character and details of the interior architecture and how they will interact with fabrics, furniture, and wall treatments to reinforce the atmosphere. And I am just as conscious of how the landscape around a house will relate to its overall design, from the sense of anticipation as you approach to how the rooms will relate to the surrounding spaces outdoors. At my firm, we take great care to reinforce the relationship between the two environments: that connection is essential to making a new house seem rooted in its setting, to giving it a sense of place, and to making it feel as if it's always been there.

Yet if people come to my firm because they love historic architecture and old houses, wanting a new or updated home that retains the character and detail of a historic structure, they also want it reworked to be more in tune with the way we live now.

That is because although my houses are steeped in a sense of history, mimicking historic models exactly doesn't really work: in truth, life today is just too different from the times that shaped the great historic American houses we have admired so much. So although my work is deeply rooted in an appreciation for architectural traditions, it is at the same time grounded in my ambition to create environments that are comfortable and family-oriented. This is the reason that both the formal public rooms of my houses *and* their private and functional spaces demonstrate equally how tradition can still provide a dynamic setting for modern life.

As a residential architect, I believe that the highest achievement to which I can aspire is just that—creating a home. And that word *home*, to me, has everything to do with comfort, family and friends, and memories most of all. Growing up, I learned that if a house is going to feel like home, it has to create opportunities for memories, even in the smallest moments of life. That is the essence of what we do at my firm and what I hope you will take with you from the pages that follow.

OPPOSITE: LEFT: Melrose Plantation, my grandmother's Georgia home, in the 1930s; the classical porte cochere had been added in the previous decade. RIGHT: My brother and I on Melrose's broad marble porch steps (that dog liked me best!). ABOVE: LEFT: Melrose's garden-facing porch connected all the wings of the house. RIGHT: The big paneled living room in the 1970s.

# PART I
## THE ELEMENTS OF A GREAT HOUSE

# ARCHITECTURE
## FINDING NEW RELEVANCE FOR TRADITION

I once had a client who told me that he wanted the floors in the brand-new classical house my firm was designing for him . . . to sag.

It was an unusual request, to be sure, but I understood. As an architect who specializes in the creation and renovation of traditional residences, my clients often nurture cherished memories of old houses, places that derived their character—proudly enduring, bent but unbowed—from the eventful passage of time. This man didn't literally want a sagging floor, but rather the feelings that such a quirk can deliver: a reassuring sense of timelessness, of the presence of history and tradition.

Not surprisingly, people who love classical architecture, with its beautifully detailed moldings and harmonious proportions, also love the idea of rooms for traditional living: a gracious entry hall in which to welcome family and friends; an elegant living room for convivial gatherings; a formal dining room perfect for candlelit dinners; and a handsomely paneled library to display a cherished collection of books. Yet as the great modern design polymath Gio Ponti once observed, "For life to be great and full, we have to combine the past with the future." Indeed, after describing their attachment to the old ways, my clients usually present a long list of

distinctly contemporary requirements: an eat-in kitchen with an adjoining family room for watching TV, a big laundry room or a gym, play spaces for the kids, and, of course, a mudroom—to name just a few.

The fact is, as our way of life has changed with time's passage, so have the nature and proportions of the spaces we inhabit. A century ago, living rooms may have been enormous, but kitchens were tiny (as they were often strictly for servants), the office was on Wall Street and not off the master suite, and gyms and media rooms were nonexistent. Today, even in classical residences, these so-called secondary spaces are where we live most of our lives—if the tail isn't quite wagging the dog, it is nonetheless just as big.

Thus the challenge, architecturally, is to retain the well-loved proportions, details, and character—the *feeling*—of a more formal, traditional residence, yet balance these elements with rooms that reflect the realities of informal twenty-first-century family life and to do so holistically, so that both aspects of a home's personality can be well integrated and enjoyed.

## A CHANGE OF PLAN

One of the most effective ways I know to contemporize a classical residence—whether we're renovating an existing historic home or starting from scratch—is to rethink the placement of rooms within the traditional plan. If in the old days (to cite one example) no one visited the kitchen and everyone gathered in the living room, today the opposite is true: living rooms are often reserved for "occasions," and kitchens—big, with breakfast tables, TVs, and sometimes even fireplaces and sofas—are the true living rooms. Given the new reality, doesn't it make sense to upend the old hierarchies and move the kitchen from its traditional exile at a

house's far corner and closer to the heart of the action?

That is precisely what we did in a classic five-part American Palladian country house my firm designed for an East Coast couple. The pair very much enjoy cooking and socializing with friends while doing so; they wisely recognized that if the kitchen were sited in a distant wing, the rest of their beautifully detailed new home would get much less use. So we placed it in the central part of the house, right off the entry hall and only steps from the living room. In terms of its architecture, detail, and material palette, the house remains unmistakably traditional, even formal, but in this respect, the plan is closer in spirit to a contemporary loft.

It is also sometimes the case that rooms once considered essential can be extracted from the plan entirely. Maid's rooms are a common example, but a pair of empty nesters for whom we worked went further and did away with the dining room too. Instead, we designed a grand and traditional living room, with a large center table that could be expanded for the occasional formal dinners the couple hosted. We also gave them a spacious kitchen/family room more suited to the informality of daily life and relaxed get-togethers with friends. Either situation on its own would have proven insufficient: like so many people who enjoy traditional living in a modern context, the couple required both.

(I should note that one of the problems of replanning an actual historic home is that its service spaces, closets, and bathrooms are usually much smaller than what we are used to nowadays, and it can be a challenge to comfortably include all of the contemporary functions our clients require. If there is a big attached garage or outbuilding near the main residence to steal space from, that can save the day; sometimes it's just a matter of reapportioning existing square footage to achieve a comfortable

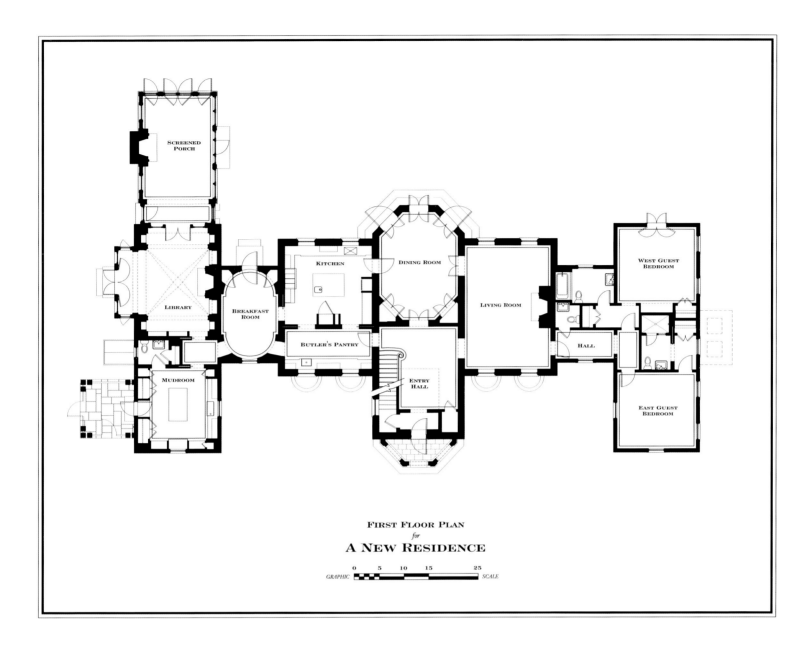

SCREENED
PORCH

LIBRARY

BREAKFAST
ROOM

KITCHEN

DINING ROOM

WEST GUEST
BEDROOM

LIVING ROOM

BUTLER'S PANTRY

HALL

MUDROOM

ENTRY
HALL

EAST GUEST
BEDROOM

FIRST FLOOR PLAN
*for*
**A NEW RESIDENCE**

0    5    10    15        25
*GRAPHIC*                      *SCALE*

balance between formal and informal areas—for example, taking over a guest room to create a large master suite.)

## GOING WITH THE FLOW

Another issue that frequently arises in traditional homes—one also related to the plan—is flow. In the wonderful early twentieth-century Colonial Revival homes we all love, there was virtually no direct communication between the back-of-house functional rooms and the more formal entertaining rooms. Now that we're spending so much time in those once-remote spaces, it is essential to create fluent connections between them and other parts of a house.

One effective means of doing so is to introduce enfilades—running, if possible, the full length of a house. These long, unbroken passageways create physical, visual, and aural connections between the formal and informal ends of a home without compromising the character or definition of the individual rooms; apart from enabling a residence's

PREVIOUS: New brass rim locks, uniquely fit with E. R. Butler's cobalt glass knobs, and traditional wood graining on the doors in my Greenwich Village apartment. ABOVE: Our plan for a new five-part American Palladian house in the Georgian style set the kitchen at the center to suit the more informal lifestyle of the clients (who love to cook and entertain).

ABOVE: Classicism can be both formal and informal. For a farmhouse in New York's Hudson Valley, we abutted a series of vernacular wings to suggest a house that had evolved over time. OPPOSITE: At the same time, formal classicism has a great deal of flexibility, as is evident in this country house façade, which applies Greek Revival details to a Palladian plan.

disparate parts to flow into one another, enfilades can also help break down the scale of even the largest house, making it feel more livable.

We also try to create rational vertical connections that facilitate upstairs/downstairs flow. I say *rational* because many of us have had the experience of wandering up a back stair in an old farmhouse, thinking we know where we're going, and getting hopelessly lost in a warren of tiny, seemingly identical rooms. That can be fun when you're a child—it's a chance to explore—but as an adult it can drive you crazy. Consequently, while we will likely always provide a grand main stair that leads from the entry hall up to the principal bedrooms (when they're on the second floor), we also often try to create a back stair that connects the kids' bedrooms with the family room and kitchen directly below, providing them with ready access to the parts of the house they use most without compromising their parents' privacy. Not as much of an adventure as the "stairway to nowhere" of the past, I grant you, but far more user- and family-friendly.

Lastly, however much we may love tradition, we have all been exposed to modernism's legacy of openness and light, large expanses of glass that afford us wide-open views with a strong connection to nature and rooms separated by little more than floating walls. The challenge lies in achieving that welcome condition without making it look like all the windows are too big or the rooms have lost their definition. We raise door headers and enlarge openings between rooms to introduce a sense of spaciousness and connectedness without pulling apart the proportions that give classical architecture its special distinction. And we also give careful attention to

the scale and detail of windows and French doors in a façade, to increase exposure to the outdoors without compromising the integrity of the house's traditional character.

## THINK THIN

Architects, planners, critics, and even builders and developers have decried the proliferation of the McMansion: bloated, inefficient, often tasteless monstrosities meant to cater to our belief that bigger means better. While I agree with that assessment, I have my own reason for opposing McMansions: they're too thick. As houses get thicker and thicker, with layer upon layer of rooms that can remind you of the rings of a tree, their inner spaces get farther and farther away from fresh air and natural light.

Apart from limits imposed by prevailing methods of building, historic homes were often only one room wide because, in the days before in-home electricity, their residents wanted to be exposed to the pleasures—indeed, the necessities—of cross-ventilation and sunshine. Sometimes the old ways really are the best, and a thin house remains a fundamental aspect of my sensibility.

Partly it results in a better proportioned, architecturally harmonious outcome: one of the reasons that McMansions look so bizarre is that, to span the unnaturally supersized volume of the house, the roof has to be unnaturally tall—much too tall,

PREVIOUS PAGES: Large French windows in this house's main block and wings fill the interior with light and bring the garden views inside. OPPOSITE: The spectacular Hudson Valley view, glimpsed through the French doors at the far end of this house's center hall, isn't revealed until you enter the front door.

ABOVE: The elongated Federal proportions of the entry porch columns on this new Colonial Revival farmhouse reflect its region's architectural traditions. OPPOSITE: The entry in the same house. The large brass rim lock, wrought-iron strap hinges, and wide plank floors express the Hudson Valley's Dutch Colonial architectural heritage.

ABOVE: Classicism's adaptability remains evident in the pairing of a sinuously curved Greek Revival staircase with bold, vibrant colors to convey a youthful spirit. OPPOSITE: A pine-paneled library in the same house is positioned on an enfilade extending the full length of the structure and connecting together its formal and informal spaces.

proportionally, for the height of the exterior walls. A more important reason for one-room thickness is that, in a day and age when we all want to conserve our natural resources, a house which is naturally well lit and properly ventilated—where we don't need to turn on the lights or air-conditioning all the time—is exceptionally energy-efficient. So we try to design rooms where you never feel far from the outdoors, with windows on two, or even three, sides—spaces that are, like their historic forebears, "green" by commonsense conception.

## CONTEMPORARY CLASSICISM

People sometimes ask me, "How can you design homes that are based on classical precedents when you're a twenty-first-century architect?" My answer is simple: classicism is a language, and you can speak it in a contemporary way.

Classicism, of course, allows an architect to tap into our memories of the past. But it is also timeless, because its essential principles, notably an adherence to proper proportions, never go out of style. In a well-designed classical interior, we immediately feel at home and at ease, not least because the ancient Greeks and Romans derived their architecture from the proportions of the human figure.

Another thing that's wonderful about classicism is that it makes room for an architecture that can be either formal or informal. Vernacular buildings in the American Classical style were often designed and built by the amateurs who occupied them, who selected their details from eighteenth- and nineteenth-century pattern books (which showcased residential architectural elements and offered suggestions for their correct use) and then simplified them to suit their tastes and abilities as craftsmen. That means that you can have an elegantly articulated interior that's very high style

or a more humble space that draws upon the same design principles but expresses them more simply. Both are classical, and both can even coexist in the same residence: dressy and casual rooms that speak to one another in a way that's consistent, letting a home be comfortable and livable rather than museum-like.

It's also the case that classicism can connect us to traditions we love but adapt to conditions that are contemporary. By that I mean the moldings, patterns, and details comprising the language of classicism are as applicable to the design of a garage, a TV cabinet, or a kitchen island as they are to a grand living parlor or formal dining room. The vocabulary may have its origins in antiquity, but its lessons, if properly adapted, can be applied to life as we live it today.

When I attended school and studied a strictly contemporary curriculum, I was taught that architecture should express what modern life is all about—its violence, dislocations, and random juxtapositions. We never talked about what made something beautiful. But classicism *is* beautiful. It gives you a sense of well-being, and there is a solace and solidity to be found in it, all of which I find much more appropriate and appealing for a house than violence and dislocation. An architecture that perpetually reminds you of the discord of daily life may have its place, but I don't think you need to find it when you turn the key to your front door.

OPPOSITE: The slender Federal proportions of the cornice moldings paired with a Greek Corinthian column screen help tell the "story" we devised for this new house, by implying later alterations. FOLLOWING PAGES: Newly designed fireplaces in five different houses, each expressive of the particular architectural character of the room in which it's installed.

ABOVE AND OPPOSITE: Two views of the same master bath. The application of classical detailing to such quotidian objects as tub fronts and sink vanities brings scale and elegance to a mostly functional room. The shutters ensure privacy; the "floating" mirror, selected by interior designer Miles Redd, helps maximize the natural light.
FOLLOWING PAGES: Bathrooms in five of our houses, from vernacular to formal, demonstrate classicism's adaptability.

ABOVE AND OPPOSITE: The two parts of this kitchen/family room remain open to each other and to the garden just outside, reflecting our contemporary preference for informal living. The rustic beams and less formal millwork support the relaxed atmosphere.

In this vernacular country house kitchen, designed in collaboration with the decorator Michael Smith, the furniture-like cabinetry conceals most of the major appliances. FOLLOWING PAGES: A selection of details from a variety of projects demonstrates how the classical language can be deployed at multiple levels of refinement.

ABOVE: For this renovation of a lakeside cottage in Connecticut, we created a porch to tie together different parts of the house, by opening the rooms to one another and to the outdoors. OPPOSITE: A glass-enclosed porch in the Hudson Valley. In summer, you can open all the windows, while in the winter months the room still remains light, cheerful, and comfortable.

ABOVE: A carriage house on a country estate has out-swinging garage doors and a pass-through leading to the garden. The cupola brings light into the second-floor rooms. OPPOSITE: A country house mudroom, with a heated stone floor and benches for taking off your boots.

# DECORATION
## MAKING ARCHITECTURE COMFORTABLE

Though it is an exaggeration to say that, like cats and dogs, architects and decorators are always at odds with one another, it remains undeniably the case that many of the former are uncomfortable giving up authority to the latter. My own theory is that this is a legacy of architecture school, where you work by yourself on your creations, the sole author; schools also build up the cult of the "genius architect" whose vision is inviolate and sacrosanct. In fact, one of the first things I learned in the real world of day-to-day practice is that architecture is always a collaboration, with the people in one's own office as well as the many other professionals who have a role in how a project will turn out. With apologies to Ayn Rand (and her architectural alter ego, Howard Roark), there is no first-person singular in architecture, especially the residential kind that I practice, in which the presence of decoration is inevitable.

Fortunately, the decoration of houses is a natural part of my design vocabulary—growing up, my stepmother was an interior designer, and both my parents believed that proper (if not necessarily elaborate) decoration was an integral part

of creating a home. My mother, who had very specific notions about what comprised a "good" room, would take me along as a boy when she would go to pick out fabrics, and showed me why certain things went together (and others did not). My father's tastes were more urbane—he lived in an elegant Carrère and Hastings–designed Manhattan town house that was quite different from my mother's nineteenth-century farmhouse in rural New Jersey; not surprisingly, he had a lively interest in the decorative arts and antiques in particular, and we made many an excursion together to auction houses and museums. Though I chose architecture as a profession, like my grandfather, what I learned from both parents is that there is a discipline to decoration: when you walked into their rooms and looked at the fabrics, furniture, carpets, and curtains, the presence of a unifying aesthetic sensibility behind the choices was clear.

Experience has taught me something else as well: many times, a client will trust a decorator more than an architect. In my profession, we spend a lot of time thinking about how things go together structurally and functionally—we're worried about the box in a rigorous, sometimes overly disciplined way. Decorators (to borrow a useful cliché) are by contrast very adept at thinking outside the box; they're capable, in the best sense, of an undisciplined approach that can be much more fun, and introduce lively moments into a project that

PREVIOUS PAGE: The black scagliola mantel in my own Greenwich Village apartment was inspired by a plate in a nineteenth-century pattern book by Asher Benjamin. RIGHT: In the parlor of that same apartment, I added a new Greek Ionic column screen. The bookcase helps give scale and definition to the room. FOLLOWING PAGES: For a large country house living room, I created a strong architectural framework, which the client and the interior decorator Miles Redd filled with bold color and an eclectic collection of furniture.

otherwise might not be there. It's also true that many decorators enjoy beautiful lifestyles themselves, which residential clients naturally respond to out of a desire to realize something similar in their own home.

The upshot is that I am somewhat of an anomaly in my profession: an architect who tries to think like a decorator—about the ways in which people like to live, and how to make room for that within the parts of a project for which my office is responsible.

## CONSTANT COLLABORATORS

You might be surprised to learn that, as the principal of my firm and the person who guides the design of each of our projects, I can spend almost half my time working directly

with decorators and thinking about decoration—that's how significant the relationship can be. For this reason, I try to get an interior designer involved at the very beginning of a project. Good ones have great ideas, many of which will have an impact, in ways large and small, on the architecture, or sometimes even be at odds with it; if the two disciplines aren't integrated step by step—if the decorator doesn't come

ABOVE: There are two fireplaces in this new Hudson Valley farmhouse living room: one an 1820s original, the other a copy. OPPOSITE: In the same house, the library adjoining the living room features painted bookcases and a lime-washed beamed ceiling, underscoring the air of informality.

in until I'm done—either those ideas will be compromised, or they'll to some degree unravel the architecture. Conversely—and no surprise—a project in which the various parts are thoroughly, seamlessly integrated will prove much more successful than one that is at war with itself.

So, how does that process work? Typically, my office goes first, as there has to be a preliminary floor plan to which everyone can respond. Then the decorator begins to imagine how to treat the rooms. "Why don't we make the dining room completely out of mirrors?" might be one idea. Or "Let's upholster the bedroom walls." Though such small decisions might seem to impact negligibly on the architecture, the opposite is true. If the decorator wants an upholstered room, for example, we will specify deeper moldings, so that the fabric isn't bulging out past them once the upholstery is installed—a small thing, but one that ensures the room will be properly tailored.

Other ideas can affect the architect's work more dramatically. "That French door won't work with the kind of curtains I have in mind"; "the fireplace is on the wrong wall for the furniture plan"; "the view is prettier in that direction—why don't we move the master bedroom to the other side of the house?" It can be challenging at times to hear these suggestions and, to be sure, nothing proceeds without a dialogue. But the more the decorator's notions are successfully layered into our overall architectural concept, the richer and more satisfying the outcome.

I also try to remember that the decorator has a separate relationship with our mutual clients, one that may yield insights into the way they like to live that, focusing as we do on the architecture, we are not always privy to; a request for space for more comfortable dining chairs or a niche for a three-way

mirror may well be a matter of psychology, not simply aesthetics, and so we make sure to be open-minded and responsive.

## COMFORT COUNTS

It is impossible to overstate the importance of comfort to a successfully designed house. That might sound like the most obvious idea in the world, but it's one that architects can lose track of from time to time. I create homes that conform to a vision that I have developed in my mind, based on what I believe a particular building should be, and how that plays out at every scale. Though I try not to let it happen, comfort can sometimes be a casualty of a strong architectural vision. As people who deal not just with style but with lifestyle, decorators are very rigorous about insisting upon the comfort quotient, and they frequently provide an understanding into ease and livability that an architect might not always have.

Of course, interior designers, like architects, are subject to their own foibles as well, and sometimes an artful interior can end up looking more like a stage set in which every object has been perfectly selected and situated, and thus the needs of the client can become secondary. But most excel at creating welcoming places to sit, good lighting by which to read, enough surfaces to set down a drink, rooms in which a meal can be enjoyed convivially—everything you'd want and need to have a rich and fulfilling domestic life. Such considerations can also make a very classical work of architecture feel warmer—less like a museum piece, more like a fun and modern home. Or as the decorator Miles Redd (with whom I have

OPPOSITE: Layering an interior gives it a cozy, lived-in feeling. This parlor includes family photos, artworks, vases, books, flowers, and a pleasingly mismatched collection of furniture and fabrics.

LEFT: The strongly proportioned mantel that decorator David Netto designed for a Charles Platt house we restored in Nashville proved a dynamic choice for an otherwise classically "correct" room. OPPOSITE: In this New York City living room, an oversize mirror and pictures hung salon-style infuse a low-ceilinged room with a dash of grandeur.

collaborated many times over the years) puts it, "fancy but cozy" (though "elegant but cozy" would probably be my own more understated take on that motto).

## LAYER UPON LAYER

Houses work best—they feel most like homes—when the architecture is layered with everything a decorator brings to the table: furniture and fabrics, antiques and artworks, family photos, bibelots, books—all of the wonderful elements that combine to create an indelible and highly personal sense of place. And this happens most successfully when the architect and decorator can jointly develop a sensibility about the lifestyle that will be lived in the house we are creating together.

That ethos of collaboration prevailed in the design of a

New England farmhouse I worked on with the interior designer Michael Smith. Pondering possible narratives that might drive the house's design, we developed the idea that it should feel like an actual Colonial-era residence that had been redone in the Colonial Revival period of the 1930s. To support this notion, I designed bathrooms with unexpectedly generous proportions that suggested the spaces had originally been put to other uses; and then Michael subliminally underscored this idea by selecting Art Deco–style fixtures and accessories of the sort prevalent during the Colonial Revival era. Working together, we were able to achieve a hybrid sensibility, resulting in something unique yet with a comforting familiarity, like the memory of a beloved place.

As well as making us feel more rooted, layering interiors can also add an unexpected jolt of vitality, a frisson that keeps

I collaborated on this country house dining room
with interior decorator Michael Smith, who commissioned the mural depicting the surrounding countryside.
Simple moldings give the space a rural flavor, yet it
easily accommodates the sophisticated English
Regency furniture and Edwardian billiards lamp.

ABOVE: The dining room in my country house, which by day serves as a library (with books on the table). The lamps are tall enough for guests to see under during dinner and give the room a warm glow. OPPOSITE: In my New York City apartment, a similar strategy: my desk converts to a dining table.

ABOVE AND OPPOSITE: Two views of the master bedroom in my New York apartment, designed in collaboration with Miles Redd. The steel bed is a copy of a nineteenth-century campaign model; vertically striped wall upholstery and my custom-designed bookcases accentuate the space's height. In the adjoining dressing room, that height affords generous floor-to-ceiling cabinetry; antiqued mirror glass expands an otherwise narrow room.

comfort from sliding into complacency. I have seen this again and again in my projects. The decorator David Netto demonstrated his mastery of this notion in the living room of a formal historic house that we worked on together in Nashville, Tennessee. By introducing into the room a gutsy, noticeably overscale Georgian mantel, he was injecting a more modern idea about decoration than the rigorous Charles Platt interior I was suggesting. Had the decision been left to me, I probably would have designed a perfectly proportioned period mantel for the room—but it might not have had the same vitalizing zing.

On another project, in the living room of a Greek Revival home that Miles Redd and I designed for a couple with an eclectic collection of antique furniture, we created a lively, unexpected conversation between the objects in the space and the architecture that enclosed them. We began by crafting a sumptuous backdrop in the boldly scaled room with strong moldings, double fireplaces, and walls upholstered in soft green linen. Then Miles layered in our clients' eighteenth- and nineteenth-century French, Italian, and English pieces, adding a pair of mahogany Regency-style console bookcases of our own design to the mix. Art completed the conversation: Miles and the owners hung an intriguing mix that included a grouping of Piranesi engravings as well as two large-scale paintings of architectural interiors the owners commissioned for the twin mantels. With big windows that extracted the architectural period's stiffness, and a refreshing lack of overcoordination in the decorative elements, the outcome had none of the stodginess that can sometimes overwhelm a large and formal residence. While the room was still grand and elegant, our efforts made it feel loose and light-spirited as well.

## LIVING COLOR

Color is another one of the tools in a decorator's kit that can have a dramatic impact on a house's architecture, helping to create a mood, capitalizing on the light within a room, and foregrounding a project's historic character and context. All of these qualities and more came into play in my own New York apartment, where I wanted to paint the walls of the grandly proportioned, classically detailed parlor something other than the bland white they had been when I bought it. Working with the color specialist Eve Ashcraft (another longtime collaborator), we developed a perfect shade of Tuscan terra-cotta that was neither too orange nor too red, one that sets off the formal architecture (which includes strong moldings and an Ionic column screen), objects, and artworks; reduces the scale of the space, with its thirteen-foot-high ceilings, making it more enveloping; and, not least, leavens what might otherwise be a somewhat imposing space with a welcoming warmth.

All of that—and from just one color.

One of my first professional jobs after graduate school was at an architecture firm that also did interior design. One day, I showed my boss the progress on a project I'd been working on, and his slightly frustrated reaction—which I've never forgotten—took me completely by surprise. He said, "Look, just make it pretty." *Pretty* was not a word we used at architecture school, but it's one I have since made a fundamental part of my lexicon. Residential architecture is partly about solving problems and partly about finding a style that is appropriate to the tastes and needs of the residents. But it's also about creating something beautiful—a resonant background for domestic life. For many of my clients, building a home is the realization of a dream, a reflection of the way they have always imagined things would turn out. In that context, architecture is the frame around the picture (hopefully a pretty one) of life—a picture that comes alive when the architect and decorator paint it together.

OPPOSITE: In this guest bedroom in my own country house, interior decorator Miles Redd and I layered multiple patterned fabrics against one another and a background of dusty blue Donald Kaufman paint. Not only does the room demonstrate that disparate fabrics can happily coexist, it is also invested with a seemingly accidental vitality.

ABOVE: The moldings in this master suite were designed to match millwork and a mantel salvaged from a historic house. Decorator Michael Smith bound the two rooms together with an elegant Chinese scenic wallpaper. OPPOSITE: In the adjacent master bath, Michael introduced Art Deco fixtures to suggest that the original colonial-era room had been repurposed in the 1930s (while in fact the house is new).

This guest suite, the centerpiece of which is a magnificent antique bamboo bed, demonstrates how many seemingly disparate elements can be successfully intermingled by a skillful decorator (in this case, Miles Redd). The walls are covered in a fresh glazed chintz, which is counterbalanced by an antique Persian rug; the objects and artworks, though differing in style, period, and importance, complement one another; and the exuberant curtain pelmets—a Redd trademark—nicely frame the view.

# LANDSCAPE
## CRAFTING A SENSE OF PLACE

Have you ever visited someone's house in the country for the first time and enjoyed a growing sensation of wonder at what awaits at the end of that long, winding driveway? You may catch a glimpse of the house or of a special view along the way before turning again to find yourself traveling through woods, over a creek, or across a meadow. That sense of mystery and anticipation, followed by arrival, when you finally see the house in full, is one of the more special experiences you can have in a landscape—one that has a profound impact on shaping a house's unique character.

Although these journeys may at times seem like happenstance, they are often the outcome of careful forethought and planning by an architect and a landscape designer working together—one of the many gestures that connect a residence to its land. I have said that I never consider architecture apart from interior decoration, and the same is true of landscape. To me, a house and its setting are of a piece, whether the architecture is meant to evoke a kind of rambling farmhouse that has grown and evolved spontaneously over time or something more formal and deliberate. For this reason, I always believe it is important to incorporate landscape design into a project's overall budget from the outset, even if it requires scaling back on other things; I never lose sight of the fact that what we are creating is not just a dwelling but a true sense of place.

## NATURAL SELECTIONS

Often clients come to us with what I call "a cornfield and a dream"—that is, an expanse of raw land on which they hope to build a house that looks like it's been nestled on the property for decades, if not centuries. This effect is indeed possible, but to achieve it, I like to work with a landscape designer to give the area around the house structure—to create "outdoor rooms" that anchor the building to its site and allow it to become one with the land. This can involve bending a house around a court-yard; encircling it with enclosed garden spaces, lawns, and stone walls; and sometimes adding outbuildings such as a garage or garden shed—efforts that collectively turn what otherwise would have been a solitary, uncomfortably exposed structure into part of a sheltering compound. If a site happens to be blessed with a stand of old-growth trees against which a house can nestle, so much the better; if not, we might bring in some new large trees (budget permitting) to diminish the impact of the size of a house on the land, or create an orchard that extends the geometry of the architecture out into the landscape.

We will also look for ways to create explicit connections between a house and its grounds—with, for example, something as simple as French doors that open onto the lawns and gardens, or through architectural axes that extend from within the house out into the spaces surrounding it. And it is no less important to create easy, natural links between the exterior spaces them-selves, to tie them together into an entourage of individual ex-periences that collectively contribute to a sense of place. This can be achieved with even the simplest of gestures, like a path of stepping-stones set into the grass.

Just as I think about a house's material palette and how it will reinforce the controlling idea underpinning the architec-ture, the same scrutiny must be applied to the selection of plant material—to make choices that feel like they belong unreserv-edly where they are and contribute to the particular experience we're trying to achieve. The goal is to make the house feel in-evitable—as though there could not possibly have been a more perfect integration of the natural and man-made worlds.

## HAVING AN EDGE

The tension that exists between a formal landscaped garden and its wilder surroundings—and how to manage the line between them—has fascinated me since childhood. Growing up on my family's farm, and also when visiting relatives' country houses, I was struck by the transition I experienced entering a property that seemed predominantly wild and natural, then felt steadily more orderly and refined as you worked your way up the drive to the house. Finding the balance between those two realms—

PREVIOUS PAGE: A potting shed I created with landscape designer Deborah Nevins using antique building materials. The client found it so enchanting that she gives dinner parties in it as well. LEFT: Many clients come to me with raw farmland; the challenge is to create a sense of place for the house that will sit upon it. OPPOSITE: I dealt with this challenge at my own country house, in part by adding sheltering trees and creating outdoor rooms. The old Adirondack chairs provide a destination for a walk through the meadow.

celebrating that juxtaposition and defining its edges—remains one of the most intriguing aspects of landscape design to me. It is one that can give a rural property a special magic.

In my experience, there's no right or wrong way to do this. My own preference is not to create so formal a situation that your planned landscape feels alien to its natural context, but that's really a matter of taste and personality: I simply prefer understatement, especially when one of the goals is to blend in. But that doesn't mean a dramatic contrast can't, under the right circumstances, prove just as effective (as in the formal hedges at my own house)—or that you cannot dispense with the formal aspect of landscaping almost entirely. Indeed, that's what the landscape designer Deborah Nevins and I did for a new house in New York's Hudson Valley: setting the residence in the midst of a stand of existing trees, we brought the blueberry bushes from the surrounding woods right up to the motor court walls, to knit the building directly into the experience of unmanaged nature.

Nor are there any hard-and-fast rules governing *how* to draw the line. Sometimes a wall works best, other times a hedge or a grade change suffices, and occasionally it can just be a matter of how you mow or don't mow. At another house, a site with a spectacular view, we knew we wanted to have a formal lawn off the back porch—one on which people could gather without feeling unprotected, as though they were out in an open meadow—but we didn't want to divorce the experience completely from the wilder field beyond. So while our design called for a low stone wall to create an edge between the two precincts, we left a thirty-foot-wide opening in it, one that made for easy

PREVIOUS PAGES: We created a sense of place for this Hudson Valley farmhouse, set in the middle of a cornfield, by surrounding it with an entourage of landscape gestures—new trees, stone walls, outbuildings. RIGHT: Deborah Nevins and I sited this house in such a way that its magnificent view isn't revealed until you enter the front door. And Deborah brought the wild landscape of the surrounding woodlands right up to the house to give it a more naturalistic character.

78

visual (and psychological) communication between the formal and informal parts of the land, and inserted a very subtle line of paving stones between the two piers—in effect, an architectural version of a dotted line—to gently define the threshold.

And let's not forget about the edges between the spaces that collectively comprise the garden realm of a property. Hedges, walls, trees, paving—all of these and more can be used to define the related yet distinct experiences that make up a house's setting. When I built my own country house, for example, I wanted some kind of a fence to create an edge to the property and punctuate the entrance to the driveway. My first instinct was to set it right next to the country road, but Deborah Nevins, working with me on the landscape design, convinced me to push the fence back a bit instead. It was a relatively subtle move but exactly the right one; having that little bit of a buffer zone between the public and private realms makes a world of difference—something I never would have come to on my own. As in my work with decorators, I have found that a close collaboration with landscape designers yields equally unexpected and delightful surprises.

## VIEW MANAGEMENT

As my enthusiasm for a carefully choreographed approach to a house suggests, view management—the process of withholding visual revelations until precisely the right moment—remains a central component of my thinking about landscape design. To me, there is nothing more disappointing than a driveway that reveals a property's defining view before you've even arrived at the front door. Knowing that you have to be at the house itself to have this keenly pleasurable experience gives the structure ownership of the landscape it overlooks—or as the architect Robert A. M. Stern once put it, "pride of place."

Indeed, I am a great believer in sustaining a sense of discovery for as long as possible, and the surest way to do so is to withhold the full exposure of the view until you actually enter the house.

When the site conditions are right, I have worked hard to create a particular procession, one that begins with that long drive through the property, gains drama with the revelation of the house, and continues as you enter the motor court, the elements of which might conceal any hint of what lies beyond. Once inside, the entry hall can act as the threshold to the more private realm of the garden—and its view—on the other side of the house. There, you are once again reconnected with the nature of the property, but now it is framed by the architectural character of the house. The British classicist Sir Edwin Lutyens, in collaboration with the garden designer Gertrude Jekyll, was a master of this narrative, as many great residential architects have been, for the simple reason that it is a gift that keeps on giving: no matter how many times you repeat the experience, it never loses its wonder.

## HOUSE AND GARDEN

While I don't believe in micromanaging one's experience of a house or garden, I do believe that elements belonging both to architecture and nature—loggias, pergolas, pavilions, even fences—can elegantly punctuate the ways in which you experience a landscape: framing and receiving views, drawing you toward different moments within a garden, serving as transition points between one outdoor room and another. In the same way that interior architecture can be hierarchical—elaborate high-key moldings in the living room as opposed to simple vernacular elements in the kitchen—such outdoor structures can also signal degrees of importance. My own country house, for example, has an architecturally sophisticated classical pergola over the French doors that lead to the

OPPOSITE: Creating an edge for the grounds of a country house can involve a range of architectural and landscaping gambits—or be as simple as mowing a lawn up to a certain point then letting the grass grow wild beyond it.

ABOVE AND OPPOSITE: A hedged room at my own country house, constructed from twelve-foot-high hornbeam, has the abstract look of contemporary sculpture. Such formal gestures, working with walls, terraces, and hedges, can give a dramatic structure to a natural landscape.

ABOVE: The formal classical pergola over the rear French doors of my house, overgrown with wisteria, was inspired by one at architect Charles Platt's own house in Cornish, New Hampshire. OPPOSITE: A whitewashed fence encloses a kitchen garden on the house's more informal side. The same hierarchies used in architecture apply equally to landscape. FOLLOWING PAGE: Garden elements afford multiple opportunities to frame views, shape space, and create connections.

formal lawn at the rear, while a plain board fence encloses a small *potager* off the kitchen—each appropriate to its particular place in the house's environs.

On an even smaller scale, furniture and sculptural objects can subtly shape how you experience landscape around a house. A thoughtfully placed bench or pair of urns on a wall serves as a way of speaking to a visitor, of saying, "You may not have noticed it, but this is a great place to pause and appreciate the view." It's nice to have movable furniture as well—how wonderful it is to set up a table and chairs under a tree and enjoy an impromptu al fresco meal.

While the structure and furnishing of a landscape can spark the mind, it's important to remember that a garden, in large measure, is about appealing to the senses. Color, scent, and touch all contribute to our enjoyment of nature. And each of these can bring another subtle layer to the landscapes we create. My own sense of color in a garden is subdued, probably more so than in an interior—indeed, I love the way a green landscape preserves the soothing harmony I appreciate most about nature. On the other hand, I am crazy about fragrant plants around a house. Proust was right—memory resides in the olfactory nerves; when I catch the aroma of tea olive, I'm instantly transported back in time to my grandmother's porch in Georgia, and the scent of eucalyptus vividly brings back the years I lived in California. Even just the smell of grass and trees has the power to move me. If architecture can reconnect us with our memories, so too can landscape—enriching our experience of home in ways that will ultimately shape new memories in years to come.

PREVIOUS PAGE: This water feature, in a Charleston, South Carolina, garden designed by Deborah Nevins, appears to be a reflecting pool but is in fact for swimming. RIGHT: The safety fence for this swimming pool is concealed within a double layer of yew hedging. Although the hedge is clipped in a very structured and formal way, the grass makes the setting more relaxed while the wide coping stone gives the pool a tailored edge.

ABOVE AND OPPOSITE: A pergola in Nashville, Tennessee, designed to complement the Charles Platt house we restored, frames views of Gavin Duke's elegant garden design in every direction. FOLLOWING PAGES: Formal meets informal on this Arcadian Hudson Valley hilltop: an arrangement of Adirondack chairs loosely encircles a fire pit while a pair of stately eighteenth-century stone urns frames the view from the house we designed there.

# PART II
## THE STORIES OF FOUR HOUSES

# MIDDLEFIELD
## BUILDING A NEW HOUSE ROOTED IN MEMORY

About a two-hour drive north of New York City, in the Hudson Valley, is some of the most beautiful countryside I know. It is a distinctly American landscape of dairy farms and nineteenth-century houses, yet with rolling meadows separated by hedgerows of locust, oak, and maple trees that can sometimes remind you of England. It is a place in which I immediately felt at home when I first saw it as a teenager coming there to boarding school, and again when I returned to it as an adult looking for a house to escape to from the city on weekends. There is no question that I love New York City—I have called it my home for more than twenty years—but I treasure my time in the country even more.

My house there, named Middlefield for its site in the midst of a farm field, has been the catalyst for much of my thinking about traditional architecture and its contemporary possibilities: the ways in which historic models could be reimagined for the way we live now, how tapping into your memories can imbue your work with a greater resonance, and why architecture, decoration, and landscape must work together if you want to create a great American house.

PREVIOUS PAGE: The entry façade of Middlefield, inspired by Greek Revival precedent. LEFT: The old farm road that crosses a creek and disappears invitingly into a thicket of trees as it appeared when I first saw the property. OPPOSITE: The meadow at the top of that road, framed by two hillsides, immediately suggested itself as a house site.

Middlefield's beginnings were actually somewhat accidental. About seventeen years ago, I began to search for an old country house to fix up. After considering different parts of Connecticut and Pennsylvania, I found myself drawn back to Dutchess County in the Hudson Valley. Intuitively, that landscape spoke to me most clearly—it felt like home. Better still, the region had bred a particularly felicitous strain of nineteenth-century Greek Revival residential architecture: handsomely—but not extravagantly—detailed, well-proportioned homes that own a pleasing, rural-American simplicity.

For nearly three years, I spent many a weekend house hunting, but everything I came across proved either not quite right or just too expensive. And then one day, driving down a lane near a summerhouse I'd been renting, I spotted a sign that read "For sale. 45 acres." Up to that point, I'd had no intention of buying land and building a house—honestly, I didn't consider myself quite ready to take that step. But I pulled over and found myself walking along a dirt farm path that took me over a creek, through a clearing in some trees, and up into the property that rose gently across a meadow to the top of a small knoll. There I stopped and looked around. The site, a hollow of land, was nestled between a hill on one side and a wooded edge on the other. It felt protected, almost like a secret place. And I instantly thought, *Wow, this would be a wonderful site for a house.*

I purchased the land—and almost immediately started second-guessing myself. Whenever I visit a building site, I very quickly get an intuitive sense of where I think the house belongs, one derived from my belief that a structure should nestle

into its setting and feel anchored to the land. My knoll, I knew, was just such a location. But it seemed too obvious a solution, too easily arrived at—why not the very top of the property, with its potential for panoramic views? It took a long time and a fair amount of angst for me to accept that I'd been right the first time, an experience that taught me a good lesson: don't be afraid to trust your first instincts.

Picking the right spot, however, doesn't preclude the need for site work. The wonderful landscape designer Deborah Nevins, a longtime friend and collaborator, talks about the importance of creating a sense of territory—a precinct—around a house; and so she and I worked together early on to design a series of garden rooms around Middlefield, using walls, hedges, trees, and lawn terraces to mediate between the architecture of

the residence and the land's natural topography. Once the process of the house's design began, I further strengthened the indoor-outdoor connections by lining up the visual axes inside the house with different points in the garden, linkages that make the land-scaped "rooms" feel more literally a part of the interior. (No less important was the approach up to the house: while the farm path I first traversed led straight up the center of the field to the top of the knoll, I rerouted the driveway through the woods to create an arrival experience that offered glimpses of the house before fi-nally revealing it in full as you approached the motor court.)

As for my design of the residence itself, I made an intense study of the nineteenth-century pattern books used by amateur builders of the time as well as more contemporary architectural surveys of the historic regional architecture in order to better

PREVIOUS PAGES: The house as glimpsed from the beginning of the entry drive, set on the knoll in the middle of the former farm field. OPPOSITE AND ABOVE: The drive winds up the property's gentle incline before emerging from the woods and arriving at the motor court, on axis with a small barn. The land surrounding the house is terraced and forms a series of outdoor rooms shaped by stone retaining walls and hedges.

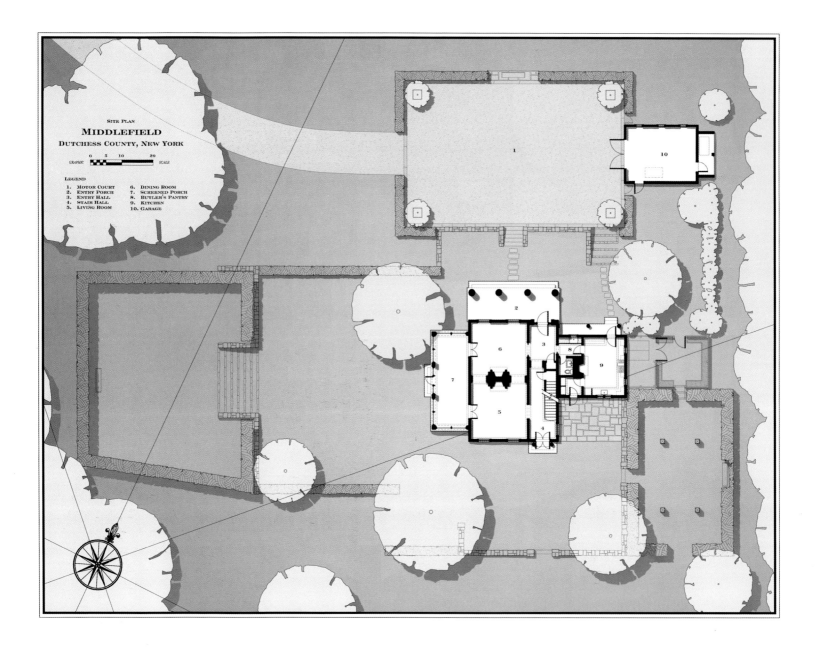

SITE PLAN

**MIDDLEFIELD**

DUTCHESS COUNTY, NEW YORK

0   5   10          20
GRAPHIC                SCALE

LEGEND

1. MOTOR COURT
2. ENTRY PORCH
3. ENTRY HALL
4. STAIR HALL
5. LIVING ROOM
6. DINING ROOM
7. SCREENED PORCH
8. BUTLER'S PANTRY
9. KITCHEN
10. GARAGE

understand the precedents. My intention was to create a classic nineteenth-century Greek Revival farmhouse featuring adjoining double parlors, with a long porch along one side of them and a stair hall running along the other, and beyond the hall, a small wing with the kitchen in it. It was to be a place imbued with the spirit of those houses I'd loved so much as a child. Additionally, I had my heart set on a double-story entry portico with hefty Doric columns, inspired by the precedent you find all over the Hudson Valley but also by a wonderful house I had seen in western Connecticut that was once home to fabric designer Alan Campbell (and now belongs to the decorator Bunny Williams). But, at the same time, I didn't want to precisely replicate the past. The challenge lay in making tradition livable: designing a home anyone would assume must be very old, yet with the sort of subtle alterations that might make it suitable for the very different way we live today.

One of my changes—perhaps the most transformative—I have already mentioned: those long axes that open up views, not only from one side of the house to the other but also to the world beyond the windows. As a result, my home never feels like a

ABOVE: The plan reveals the ways in which various landscape gestures help to frame views, knit the house into the landscape, and give Middlefield a true sense of place. OPPOSITE: Stepping stones set into the grass help to mark the entry in a more relaxed way; the clipped hedges, by contrast, impart a sense of formality.

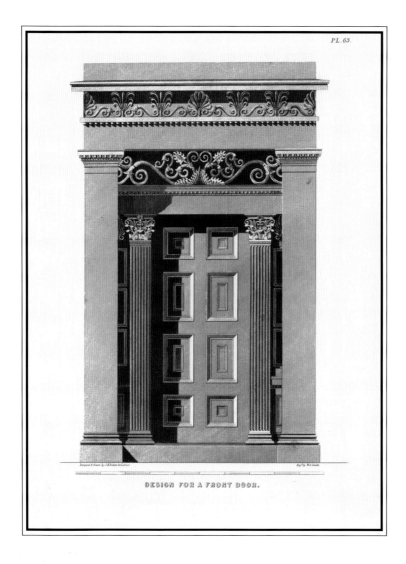

PL. 63.

DESIGN FOR A FRONT DOOR.

PREVIOUS PAGES: Multiple moments in the landscape around the house help to define its relationship to the larger natural context while treading the line between tradition and abstraction. LEFT: This plate and others, from Minard Lafever's 1830s pattern book, inspired details in my own home. OPPOSITE: Lafever's proportions influenced the design of the double-story entry portico and the entry door surround.

series of enclosed rooms divorced from one another or from their collective surroundings, but rather responds to our contemporary affection for natural light, long views, and open-plan living. This strategy proves especially effective in the entry. In older houses, typically the stair comes down toward the front door. Here, however, I flipped it, so that the upper floors are accessed from the rear of the house. Partly this was meant to give more privacy to the upstairs, where the bedrooms are located. But it also enabled me to create an unimpeded cross-axis, with sight lines from the front to the back door in one direction and from the kitchen to the dining room and adjoining screen porch in the other. The result is that when you step into the entry, you can immediately grasp the layout of the entire house and its relationship to the gardens.

Another change involved the back-to-back parlors. Of-

ten these identically sized spaces are connected via a single large archway with pocket doors, which makes them agreeably open to one another but reduces the possibility of privacy or sense of discovery and diminishes the distinctiveness of each individual room. Instead, I put two smaller (but still generous) openings on either side of the common wall, with back-to-back fireplaces in the middle, to create greater differentiation while still preserving—even promoting—fluid circulation between the rooms.

Certain alterations are practically undetectable yet deliver substantial impact. Windows are larger in scale and begin closer to the floor, so that the connection to the garden feels more immediate. The French doors leading to the screen porch remain identical in proportion to their historic predecessors yet are slightly wider, so that one can open a single door leaf and pass

ABOVE AND OPPOSITE: Upon entering the house, you find a cross-axis that affords views out into the landscape in all directions. French doors at the hallway's far end are drawn from childhood memories of the same space at Melrose, my grandmother's house. Here, the ticking of the old hall clock, which chimes on the hour, never fails to trigger similar memories of that beloved place.

ABOVE, OPPOSITE, AND FOLLOWING PAGES: The living room mantel, one of a pair (the second stands on the other side of the wall), came out of a Greek Revival house that was being torn down—I purchased it before I'd finalized Middlefield's plan, yet it proved to be a perfect match. The broad, high doorways and ten-foot ceilings make the relatively small room feel more spacious, and the tall windows never fail to flood the room with natural light. The slightly mismatched furniture and fabrics, cobbled together from antiquing expeditions and things I inherited, give the room a relaxed air.

The screened porch, on the house's western side,
is in effect an indoor/outdoor living room and
remains in near-constant use in the warm months.
I furnished it like a proper room, with old wicker
and a real upholstered sofa, after spending time on
Bunny Williams's delightful porch in Connecticut.

ABOVE: From the entry hall, one can look through the library/
dining room to the screened porch and, beyond it, into
the garden. OPPOSITE: An inexpensive table, made for the
room and covered in felt, serves as a big library table during the
day but easily transforms into a festive dining table at night.

I loved the Geoffrey Bennison fabric which covers the walls of my bedroom, but at first I rather timidly planned to use it only on a piece of furniture—until Miles Redd suggested that I put it on the walls (which has the rather delightful effect of making you feel like you're in the treetops). I found the nineteenth-century American carved bed in upstate New York; the portrait of the duke hung over the living room mantel at Melrose (although I removed its old gilt frame to make the painting look less pompous).

ABOVE: The wainscoting and painted floor in a guest bathroom reinforce the sense of being in a country house. I used an old mirror to create the medicine cabinet's door. OPPSOITE: Artful decorative touches—in this case, the Colefax and Fowler wallpaper from Bowood House in England—can effectively elevate the simplest spaces, such as this guest bedroom tucked under the eaves above the kitchen.

through without brushing one's shoulders, a lesson learned from the American classical architect Charles Platt. I set the ceilings higher than is usual for a country farmhouse—ten feet on the first floor, just under nine feet on the second—and they combine with the double-story portico to make the 3,500-square-foot house feel larger than it is. As for that portico, I elongated its proportions just a bit from some of the precedents I had studied, so that the second-floor windows facing it have unobstructed long views (and so the attic above can be experienced as a comfortably habitable space, despite the peaked ceiling).

As the saying goes, it all adds up. The classical language of the Greek Revival style remains intact, yet the house is as light, airy, open, and connected to nature as the most contemporary of dwellings. I notice it especially on hot summer days when, with the doors and windows open, the multiple axes draw a fresh, cool breeze through the rooms. The house has air-conditioning, but I've only used it three times in fourteen years.

A word about the house's decoration: growing up, I was very fortunate to be exposed by my family to some wonderful houses and rural places and to have been able to experience the ways in which the previous generations lived in them. My grandparents' generation had a talent for enjoying life: they had great traditions of hospitality and an energetic appreciation of beautiful things. They loved to collect furniture, art, and objects—sometimes "important" things, but not always. Rather, they looked for special things whose value was derived from the pleasure they bestowed upon the beholder—and because they made life more fun. In a way that sometimes seems lost to us today, that generation really knew how to *live*, and it made a strong impression on me.

When the decorator Miles Redd and I began our collaboration on the design of Middlefield's interior, it was important to me to try and capture that spirit: to imbue my house with both history and memory, which are, in fact, not quite the same thing. The former developed more from the architecture: the kitchen wing, for example, has lower ceilings, simpler moldings, and beadboard on the walls, as though it were the more modest original structure built in the eighteenth century before prosper-

ity made possible the grand Greek Revival addition. Building materials, too, play their part, such as the 150-year-old heart pine floorboards and antique glass panes in the kitchen cabinets.

Bringing memory into the design process perhaps required more delicacy. I wanted the house to feel like those of my youth, and certainly there are countless things I inherited in every room serving as touchstones from the past. Yet more important than the objects themselves is the sensibility that was passed down to me: the lack of pretension and love of beauty that, to me, finds perfect expression in those wonderful English country houses that are filled with an eclectic array of things picked up here and there, none of it matching yet somehow all of a piece. My parents and grandparents shared that approach to interior design, but their style was more buttoned-up. Years of work with many talented decorators have taught me that even the most elegant room can exude a relaxed, throwaway quality—an appealing informality. Collaborating with Miles allowed me to create my own version of my family's sensibility: to make choices that captured that spirit of their style yet still felt uniquely my own.

I hadn't initially set out to design and build my own home, but I am enormously grateful that things turned out that way. The process enabled me to test my belief that tradition can be livable—that I might create an "old" house in a beloved classical style but which, in every way, belongs to its own time. I had the opportunity to reimagine and reinterpret the domestic world of my childhood, to make it relevant yet still familiar. And aided by the talent and encouragement of Deborah, Miles, and other collaborators with whom I've worked now for many years, I was able to combine architecture, interior design, and landscaping in a way that feels inevitable, as though the house had always been, and belonged, where it is.

Most of all, I am grateful, at Middlefield, to feel so at home.

OPPOSITE: The deep proportions of the Greek Revival entablature and cornice on the exterior facilitated a full-height attic, where I installed my studio. The bold scale of the architecture also enabled me to incorporate a dramatic fanlight window that is more than six feet in width.

ABOVE: The kitchen, situated in a side wing of the house, is accessed via informal grass steps that contrast with the more "serious" stone staircase leading to the main entrance. OPPOSITE: A fireplace—always a warm and welcoming element in a kitchen—features a traditional Dutch oven door on one side. A pantry brimming with bowls, baskets, and candlesticks serves the kitchen and the terrace just outside.

Despite the pleasures of my attic studio, I actually enjoy working at the kitchen table in front of the fireplace most of all, in a room that is flooded with natural light from three sides. Antiqued brass hardware, a painted floor, and green canvas shades reinforce its casual country character.

ABOVE: A rear view of Middlefield from the meadow to the south of the house. OPPOSITE: An arched arbor frames a view of the tiny kitchen garden and, beyond it, the barn in the motor court. An urn overflowing with hydrangeas anchors the small space and is a focal point from out in the garden.

# LONGFIELD
## TELLING A STORY WITH ARCHITECTURE

As I discovered from my work on Middlefield, giving a new house a sense of place and of history is all about how effectively you handle its siting and the degree to which you imbue the architecture with an authentic character. So it was for my clients, avid horseback riders with three young children, who'd found a spectacular three-hundred-acre expanse of farmland not far from my own Dutchess County residence. They wanted to create a family retreat, from which to enjoy the countryside and the equestrian activities their farm afforded—a place with a deliberate, easygoing relationship to the land and a strong aesthetic connection to the historic houses they'd grown to love. Seeing my home had encouraged them to believe that a "new old house" was indeed possible. And for me, Middlefield proved to be an excellent warm-up for this project: the challenges posed by Longfield Farm, as they chose to call it, were actually quite similar to those I'd encountered with the design of my own place but of far greater complexity and scale.

This was especially the case with the site. At Middlefield, though I had struggled with where to place the house, my forty-five mostly untamed acres held a number of advantages: an old farm road that could be rerouted to form a dramatic approach; a variance of topography alternating between relatively level clearings and

sheltering hillsides, creating a natural hollow of land; and big, old trees against which a house might nestle. Longfield, conversely, was just as the name implies: acre upon acre of open farmland—much less hilly, with trees only at the hedgerows separating the fields. Considering it for the first time, that intuitive sense of place I had experienced on my own land was utterly absent. How, I wondered, could I make a house feel like it really belonged here, rather than as if it was simply dropped onto a vast expanse of acreage, suburban-development style?

Collaborating again with the landscape designer Deborah Nevins, we conceived the idea of a compound: a main house surrounded by landscaped exterior spaces, outbuildings, and gardens, dissolving gently into rolling fields of paddocks on one side and an apple orchard on the other—an entourage of architectural and landscape gestures that anchor the entire composition to the site. As the place we all selected for the house is on a gentle slope, Deborah wisely suggested setting the compound slightly below the grade of a nearby hedgerow, the better to create a sense of enclosure. As a result, after circling gently up from below the horse barns and paddocks on a new road, experiencing the pleasure of gradually discovering the house, and driving into the entry court, one encounters wide grass-covered steps leading up to the orchard on one side and, on the other, an entry garden set a few steps below the motor court. Rather than feeling exposed, the first impression is one of a protected, welcoming enclave rooted snugly to its spot.

That motor court is framed on two sides by the L-shaped residence, with the main residential wing along the entry garden to the left and a secondary wing containing the kitchen, mudroom, and garages directly in front of you (a stone gardener's shed anchors the fourth corner of the court). Beyond the secondary wing, Deborah and I created an arrangement of garden and service spaces that further reinforce Longfield's strong sense of place. Off the garages, we placed an

expansive service court, itself enclosed on three sides by hedges of nine-foot-tall hornbeam, and just past it—flanking the service road that forms a secondary approach to the house—a vegetable garden, a gazebo, and a swimming pool whose safety fence is gracefully concealed within a double-sided yew hedge. Deborah and I also added a final, nearly immaterial layer to loosely define the precinct of the formal lawns from the property's wilder meadows, paddocks, and fields: a low, porous stone wall built of the same warm Connecticut fieldstone from which the house and other outbuildings were constructed.

It is important to add that although we worked hard to enable the house and the garden spaces that immediately surround it to take firm ownership of the site, we worked equally hard to find ways for Longfield to become part of those three hundred acres. This effort finds its primary expression in the design's great cross-axis: the main and service roads that pass directly through the property moving east and west and the visual axis that travels north and south from the grass-covered orchard steps, across the motor court and entry garden, and on through the front and back doors of the residence. These axes connect you to Longfield's larger context. For a house to become one with the land requires more than just hunkering down on a sheltering spot—it must also reach out to, and invite in, the beautiful vistas and natural elements that are a country home's true reason for being.

The second challenge—giving the residence the character of a historic American structure rather than a McMansion—was also one I had tackled at Middlefield. Investing such a place with authenticity, I'd discovered, requires more than being able to speak the design language of classicism (though that is, of course, essential). What can also be important is the creation of a narrative—a mythology—for a home and how it evolved over time, to give shape and direction to the architecture. If you can imagine a credible backstory about the house's

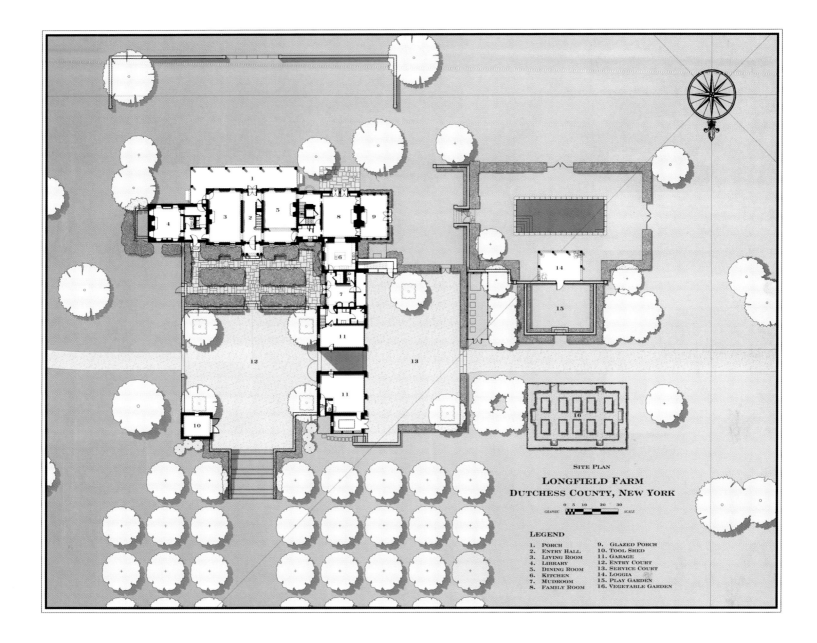

SITE PLAN

**LONGFIELD FARM**
**DUTCHESS COUNTY, NEW YORK**

0   5   10      20      30

GRAPHIC ▨▨▨▨▨▨ SCALE

LEGEND

1. PORCH                9.  GLAZED PORCH
2. ENTRY HALL          10. TOOL SHED
3. LIVING ROOM         11. GARAGE
4. LIBRARY             12. ENTRY COURT
5. DINING ROOM         13. SERVICE COURT
6. KITCHEN             14. LOGGIA
7. MUDROOM             15. PLAY GARDEN
8. FAMILY ROOM         16. VEGETABLE GARDEN

history—how it was built and lived in and what stylistic changes were made as the residence expanded—the outcome can be as complete and convincing as any well-told tale. All the details will contribute to the success of the whole; nothing will seem forced, inappropriate, or out of character.

Writing Middlefield's story was relatively easy, for the simple reason that it was my own house: I wanted to re-create some of the way of life I'd experienced in the wonderful family homes of my childhood and also explore the Greek Revival style I had gotten to know while studying the Hudson Valley. Developing Longfield's mythology required more imagination. My

clients' requirements and aesthetic preferences—as well as their personalities—naturally set the direction. But how to bring them together in a historic home that genuinely belonged to the land and community?

Our solution was to imagine that the formal residence my clients requested had been built in stages—like

PREVIOUS PAGE: Longfield's walls are made of granite fieldstone cut to emphasize horizontality. The stone gives the house an elegance without being too formal. ABOVE: The plan illustrates the organizing elements that surround the house, among them two motor courts, a pool, and an orchard.

many such vernacular farmhouses—by a gentleman farmer and his descendants in the late eighteenth and early nineteenth centuries. It would have begun modestly as a small structure in the late Colonial period (into which we put the library and part of the master suite). In the ensuing decades, a larger, more grand house (containing Longfield's public rooms below and bedrooms on the second floor) was appended to the original: sympathetic in style, but reflecting the farm's prosperity and the family's growing size. At some point in the nineteenth century, carriage barns (the garages, with guest and playrooms above) were put up and connected to the house by an open porch that, at a later date, was glassed in (the mudrooms, located between the garages and kitchen). Finally, well into the Greek Revival period, Longfield received its crowning flourishes in the form of an elegant entry portico of Ionic columns surrounding the front door and a long, slightly asymmetrical back porch, its roof supported by strong, simple Greek Doric columns.

The interior contributed to the story as well, with elements and details that reinforce both the house's classical architecture and the path of its gradual expansion. We began, as I often do, by thinking about the mantels, knowing that they would guide our designs for the moldings, cornices, and baseboards (elements so important to articulating the individual rooms). We wanted actual antique mantelpieces native to the Hudson Valley, and early in the design process we discovered two—for the living and dining rooms—dating from the 1820s, which seemed entirely appropriate for an old farmhouse. (I should add that, as they were a bit dressy, we constructed the firebox surrounds and hearths from a contrastingly humble an-

tique brick.) With the mantels as our aesthetic compass, we crafted Federal-style moldings, doors, and a beautiful "period" staircase. The house's imagined history equally influenced our material choices. The library is paneled in plain knotty pine: mahogany, or even oak, would have been much too fancy for a farmhouse, even an elegant one.

And we also deliberately incorporated the sort of accidental oddities that turn up in structures that grew over time. The doorways between the "original" building and its grander successor are extra thick to express the idea that they are piercing what had once been an exterior stone wall. In keeping with its history, we gave the "older" part of the house its own door and a small entry hall, which serves as a transitional zone between living room and library—perhaps an extravagance of space, but one that makes you feel, on a subliminal level, the structure's evolution. Another instance: the bathroom in the guest suite is a bit bigger than absolutely necessary, as bathrooms in older houses were typically fitted into small rooms to which plumbing had been added. It's quirky, I know, but without the quirks, the residence would not feel as authentic.

Typically we collaborate with an interior designer on the decoration of a house; in this case, our clients had substantial furnishings and collections already—including English and American sporting pictures, similar to those that surrounded

PREVIOUS PAGES: Views of Longfield from its planted fields; across the motor court from the orchard; and of the carriage house, stone garden shed, and mudroom connector between the carriage house and the kitchen wing. OPPOSITE: Longfield's Ionic entry porch. At the other end of the center hall, the view awaits.

me growing up—and so they wanted us simply to help them select fabrics and wallpapers and make rooms that both reflected their interests and tastes and contributed to the story begun by the architecture. One of my favorite examples of this is the hand-painted de Gournay scenic paper in the dining room. In my mind, Longfield's "original" residents became world travelers at some point and decided that they would have a scenic paper made depicting their nineteenth-century voyage to India. My clients agreed that this was appropriate to the house's mythology as well as to their own lives; we had de Gournay custom-craft a design in sepia to make it seem original to the room and add a warm glow to candlelit dinner parties. (At the opposite end of the decorative spectrum, some of the bathroom floors were painted, as this is a treatment often found in old vernacular farmhouses. Though not as grand as de Gournay, the painted floors were every bit as important to the authenticity of the design.)

Of course, this isn't the nineteenth century, and though the design speaks of the past, it also had to function well for a young, very contemporary family. Thus the plan, in one respect, is surprisingly modern: tall, wide openings on both sides of all the public rooms facilitate easy circulation and intercommunication, making a big house feel as graspable and fluent as a loft; these long enfilades, moreover, connect visually and actually to windows and doors, so that light,

In the house's "story," the smaller wing at the far left was the original house, with the larger structure following several decades later. The entry garden, three steps below the motor court, helps to make the house feel more snugly tied to the land and forms a barrier between the cars and the domestic realm of the residence.

air, and the natural world are ever present. The grand main stair rises upward from the entry hall to the adults' private quarters; a second, back stair leads down from the children's bedrooms and playroom to the family room and kitchen, so that the kids can have morning fun without waking their parents. The formal dining room can seat at least sixteen, but there are multiple places for more familial, al fresco meals: the patio off the family room, a screened outdoor porch (with fireplace), and the big back porch with its long views. As my clients are frequent entertainers, the bar communicates with the living room, library, and porch; the butler's pantry, between the dining and family rooms, does double duty as a serving station and china repository as well as a quick place for kids to grab a soda. There are even his-and-hers mudrooms—with heated stone floors for winter walking in stockinged feet.

Our efforts at verisimilitude extended to the extensive wine cellar, where we used reclaimed ceiling timbers and rough stone walls to suggest the foundations of the farmhouse (a cozy space that's also humidity- and temperature-controlled to protect its contents). The atmosphere there is so convincing that the family's children refer to it as "the dungeon."

I mentioned that my clients asked me to design Longfield after seeing my own home. What attracted them was not so much the style but the *sensibility* at work in my house; the idea that a classical residence could be habitable in a modern way. For the two to integrate seamlessly, an architect must take every aspect of a project into account: architecture, landscape, decoration, tradition. For this family, the outcome has brought a wonderful new dimension to their lives—and the "old" house of which they'd always dreamed.

LEFT: A detail of the main stair's slender Federal-style balusters and stringer brackets. OPPOSITE: The walls are covered in blocks of paper made from bark, applied so as to give the look of ashlar stone.

ABOVE AND OPPOSITE: The large living room stretches the full width of the house and is anchored at its midpoint by a handsome 1820s mantelpiece, which was found at the start of the project; the antique brick firebox surround is well suited to a country farmhouse and makes the grand space feel less formal. The beautiful antique Sultanabad carpet, another of the clients' first purchases for the house, inspired the room's color scheme.

ABOVE: The thick stone walls facilitated paneled jambs at the windows, which contribute to a sense of age and solidity. OPPOSITE: The details of the Federal-era Hudson Valley mantelpiece influenced the design of the moldings throughout the house.

ABOVE: Broad, tall openings between the rooms give the house an airy quality and create an easy flow from one end to the other. Tall French doors bring in ample light. OPPOSITE: A second antique mantelpiece graces the dining room, which features a sepia-toned scenic wallpaper by de Gournay depicting scenes of India.

ABOVE: The abbreviated hallway connecting the living room to the library, in Longfield's smaller wing, includes a second front door to suggest that this was the house's original entry. OPPOSITE: The library is paneled in a waxed pine typical of early country houses in the region.

ABOVE: The tub niche in the wife's master bath features concealed cabinets, at left and right, for towels. We designed the sink stand to resemble a piece of furniture. An antique mirror forms the front of the medicine cabinet. OPPOSITE: A cheerful printed linen from Robert Kime enlivens the bedroom in the master suite, where we installed another antique mantel.

PREVIOUS PAGES: The view from the upstairs hall into the master suite vestibule; a guest bedroom hung with an English sporting picture. ABOVE: The back stair leads up from the family room to a children's play area. OPPOSITE: A vertically striped wall fabric gives height to a child's bedroom tucked under the eaves.

ABOVE: The house's media equipment is concealed in a cabinet we designed at the foot of
the back stair between the dining and family rooms. OPPOSITE: The family room features
a more relaxed treatment, with painted paneling, a rustic beamed ceiling, and a fireplace
surround made from the same granite as the exterior. The room opens onto a dining terrace to
the south and a screened and glassed-in porch on the other side of the fireplace to the west.

OPPOSITE AND ABOVE: The capacious kitchen opens directly into the family room on one side and into the connector containing Longfield's his-and-hers mudrooms on the other. The cheerful room receives natural light throughout the day; contemporary stools modeled on comb-back Windsor chairs at the island are well suited to the house's traditional character.

ABOVE: The husband's mudroom contains a large soapstone sink for washing off boots and an area for feeding the family's dogs. OPPOSITE: The cabinetry in the wife's mudroom is more refined. The flagstone floors are heated to warm stockinged feet in the cold months.

ABOVE: A view over the vegetable garden toward the rear of the stone pool cabana and the valley the property overlooks. OPPOSITE: The Doric columned porch on the house's south side forms a transitional space between the interior and the outdoors, deep enough for seating groups and dining tables on summer evenings. The stone wall in the foreground loosely defines the edge of the formal lawn.

ABOVE AND OPPOSITE: The wood roof shingles and battens are revealed through the framing of the simple pool cabana. OVERLEAF: The view from Longfield's back porch, overlooking the formal lawn and, beyond it, the horse paddocks. A threshold of bluestone flagging at the opening in the wall gently marks the line between the formal lawn and the meadow beyond.

# BOXWOOD
## MAKING A GRAND OLD HOUSE LIVABLE AGAIN

I have talked about some of the challenges inherent in designing a new home that will suit the way we live today yet at the same time feel traditional: the need to speak the language of classicism in a modern fashion, and to develop a credible mythological history for a house that can infuse its architecture with authenticity. Redesigning an actual historic residence—in this case Charles Platt's Boxwood, completed in 1915—poses precisely the opposite problem: introducing modernity into environments that were designed to facilitate very different, and now largely outmoded, styles of living.

Why contemporize a classic? In fact, many of my clients possess conflicting sensibilities. On the one hand, they are attracted, as I am, to the formal elegance the very best old houses seem to exude without effort, a quality that draws us back magically to a more gracious, bygone era. At the same time, families today, especially if the children are young, want to be able to live comfortably and casually—and in rooms that were much more formal a century ago than their present-day counterparts. The idea, from a design perspective, is to interlace old-world elegance and contemporary informality so that the two don't fight one

another. Boxwood's reinvention captures the complexity of the task—one that in this instance embraced architecture, scholarship, reconstruction, landscape, and decoration.

The residence, in a pastoral suburb of Nashville, had several lives before I made its acquaintance. I would characterize Platt's six-bedroom original, for a well-to-do doctor client, as a Georgian farmhouse—handsome but by no means grand, understated in detail, and clad in tall shingles painted a pale gray. It was a classic early twentieth-century country residence, featuring a library in the center behind the entrance hall, a drawing room to one side, and a dining room to the other—all what you would expect to find. Yet Platt had connected the house wonderfully to its surroundings, with a row of tall French doors that opened to the garden in back and a loggia on the western end, also with French doors on three sides, that captured both the abundant sunlight and the cooling breezes so valued in an era before air-conditioning.

In the 1950s, the house received a substantive makeover from new owners, who wished to invest it with a greater measure of grandeur—most dramatically, with a double-height Corinthian portico added to the entry façade. In front and back, the shingled central portions of the façades were reclad in red brick; many of the garden-facing French doors were eliminated; and the library received a bow-fronted bay with two smaller doors. At the house's eastern end, the owners also constructed a flat-roofed, freestanding five-car garage, which eventually was connected to the residence via a large kitchen and breezeway; two protruding porches at either end, one glazed, the other open, were also added.

The house's interior received a no less transforming renovation, one that replaced a deliberately understated, classically articulated design scheme with very grown-up, dressy entertaining spaces finished in French and English overtones. The change was most evident in the entry hall, which the owners dramatically enlarged by removing the discreet enclosed stair and replacing it with a grand, curving one that swept down from the upstairs landing and arrived at the front door; large panels of plate mirrored glass and pilasters took the place of Platt's original painted paneling.

Interestingly, my clients—a young couple with three small children—had a familial and sentimental connection to the house: the husband's grandfather had been in business with the family that had owned Boxwood previously. As a re-

sult, he harbored happy memories of time spent in what became, following that 1950s renovation, one of Nashville's architectural grandes dames. Although my clients had originally planned to build a new home in the countryside, they ultimately decided to remain closer to the city, ideally with enough land around them for their kids to throw a ball without sending it through a neighbor's window. Thus Boxwood met their needs on multiple levels, and they loved the idea of making a

PREVIOUS PAGE: The oculus window in the tympanum of Boxwood's new entry portico. The window pockets up into the wall.
OPPOSITE: A photograph of the house, by architect Charles Platt, after its completion in 1915. ABOVE: Boxwood prior to its restoration, showing the entry portico and brick façade, both added in the 1950s.

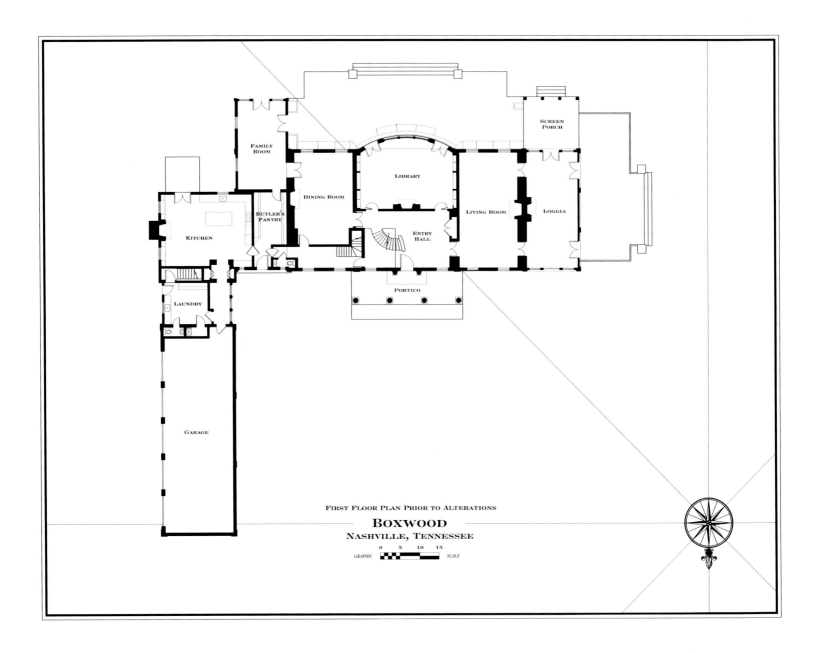

FIRST FLOOR PLAN PRIOR TO ALTERATIONS

**BOXWOOD**

NASHVILLE, TENNESSEE

0   5   10   15

GRAPHIC                    SCALE

contribution to the house's long history.

Yet while the couple was extremely enthusiastic about the place, they felt something wasn't quite right about it, although they couldn't pinpoint exactly what the problem was. Certain things, of course, were evident to us all: the architecture had wandered far afield of Platt's vision and begged to be returned to its original character; and the décor, established in the 1950s, wasn't appropriate for a young cosmopolitan couple in the twenty-first century.

But there remained a larger issue requiring a more substantive intervention. As it happened, I had met my clients years earlier, having designed a home for the husband's parents while working for another firm. I'd witnessed how important a sense of family was to the entire clan: they had long-standing ties to their community, lived in close proximity to one another, and didn't find forty people around the Thanksgiving dinner table to be the least unusual. My clients' lives, I knew, were focused on relatives, friends, and children—elegant and sophisticated, to be sure, but equally about Super Bowl parties, Sunday barbecues for nieces and nephews, and, most of all, enjoying one another's company in comfortable, unconstrained ways.

The problem was that Boxwood had been designed for a historical moment in which well-to-do families were looked after by staff, and there remained a strong separation between serving

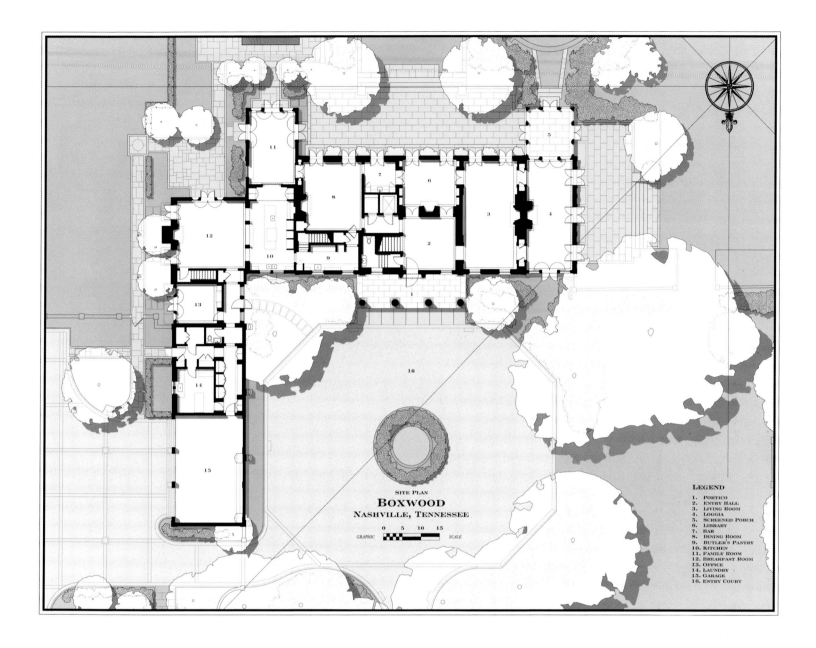

SITE PLAN
# BOXWOOD
NASHVILLE, TENNESSEE

GRAPHIC 0 5 10 15 SCALE

LEGEND

1. PORTICO
2. ENTRY HALL
3. LIVING ROOM
4. LOGGIA
5. SCREENED PORCH
6. LIBRARY
7. BAR
8. DINING ROOM
9. BUTLER'S PANTRY
10. KITCHEN
11. FAMILY ROOM
12. BREAKFAST ROOM
13. OFFICE
14. LAUNDRY
15. GARAGE
16. ENTRY COURT

and served spaces. As only household employees ventured into the kitchen—a room that today is the very center of family life—it was typically small, utilitarian, and drab. And as domestic life at the turn of the twentieth century was itself a more formal affair, the big intercommunicating breakfast and family rooms that today are indispensable were essentially nonexistent. For Boxwood to work for my clients, we had to create these informal gathering areas and get the life around them exactly right.

Just as important was the need to rethink the plan: to break down the architectural barrier between the front- and back-of-house zones that was, in Platt's day, de rigueur. If we couldn't find a way to make clear, natural connections between the "public"

living and dining rooms and the relaxed family zone, the more formal rooms would never get used—they'd end up like the embalmed, do-not-touch parlors in your grandmother's house, reserved for important guests, Thanksgiving turkeys, and Christmas trees.

We pursued the architectural battle to transform the house on two fronts. To make it more family-friendly, we returned

PREVIOUS PAGES: A view of the restored house. The Georgian door surround is original to the 1915 house. LEFT: A plan showing Boxwood as we found it, illustrating the structure's isolation from the garden and the lack of flow between service spaces and formal rooms. ABOVE: Our redesign connected Boxwood to the outdoors and facilitated a lifestyle in which the kitchen and informal family rooms would be of central importance.

PREVIOUS PAGES: The new entry hall, with Platt's restored paneling, the door heads raised up, and decorator David Netto's bold "shaded-block" floor; the living room, once again open to the garden via French doors. ABOVE: The split Ionic pilaster motif flanking the living room doors was favored by Platt but is more formal than the original house's detailing. OPPOSITE: A Giacometti lamp and a work by Andy Warhol mix in well with the dining room's more traditional elements.

OPPOSITE: A dramatic classical bust introduces a somewhat tongue-in-cheek moment into the bar. The view reveals the enfilade along the house's rear, linking the library, living room, and loggia. ABOVE: A detail of the hand-gouged oak paneling in the library, inspired by a Jean-Michel Frank console cabinet, which gives a contemporary spin to an otherwise traditional room.

PREVIOUS PAGES: Tall new pairs of doors open the library to the entry hall and create a connection between the front and rear of the house. RIGHT: I initially questioned David's desire to introduce cola-colored walls into the loggia, but they proved to be a decorative triumph. We restored several French doors that had been removed and added a boldly patterned limestone and oak floor.

the kitchen to its original location and established it as the large hub between the new family and breakfast rooms, opening up the three spaces to one another to facilitate connection. As well, we took over two of the existing garage bays and used them to create a big mudroom/home office/laundry zone that could be easily accessed from the garage and the informal family areas of the house. The library, originally as big as the living room, got smaller, so that we could insert a bar (open to the rear terrace) and a new elevator up to the third floor, formerly a warren of confining attic spaces that we converted into a playroom and suite of guest rooms. And we removed what I came to call the *Days of Our Lives* staircase (which, admittedly, had become a much-beloved fixture of the neighborhood, no doubt for its entrance-making possibilities) and installed one modeled on Platt's original, which ascends to a second family room: a gathering place for games and TV watching between the children's and parents' bedrooms. What had been a very formal residence now had multiple informal get-together zones, public and private, on every level.

There remained the need, on the main floor, to connect the "serious" rooms with their easygoing counterparts, so as not to have a house divided. To do so, I used one of my favorite gambits: long enfilades along the front and back, which open up the rooms to each other; indeed, on Boxwood's garden-facing elevation, you can stand in the loggia and see through the living room, library, bar, and dining room all the way to the family room at the house's opposite end. We also moved the library fireplace slightly to create a clear and immediate cross-axial connection: stepping in the front door, one can look straight through the entry hall and library to the garden. That link to the outside remained no less important, so we restored all of the original French doors: the house had become

LEFT: The original enclosed stair was replaced in the 1950s by what I referred to as the house's *Days of Our Lives* staircase. OPPOSITE: Our renovation replaced it with a variation on Platt's 1915 design; the damask wall fabric that David Netto installed lightens the mood.

ABOVE AND OPPOSITE: A new second-floor family room overlooks the staircase and shares its printed linen walls. The space sits between the parents' and children's wings and incorporates a spirited mix of modern and traditional elements.

RIGHT: The master bedroom, with a bed canopy in the manner of David Hicks, is enveloped in an Indian print fabric. A pair of Art Deco chests flanks the door to the master bath. The black painting above the bed introduces a note of the unexpected.

PREVIOUS PAGES: In the wife's bath, we floated a mirror in front of a
window, creating privacy as well as functionality without sacrificing
natural light. The room's paneling conceals an abundance of storage.
ABOVE AND OPPOSITE: A boy's study area and plaid-papered bathroom.

ABOVE: A series of small rooms on the house's attic level were combined to create a loftlike play space and media room. The traditionally detailed stair (which winds its way through the children's wing and down to the kitchen) is encased here in a modern wrapper in keeping with the design of the room. OPPOSITE: A girl's bedroom with a cozy reading nook—another of the personalized spaces David and I designed for each of the children's rooms.

ABOVE: A butler's pantry—a staple of a 1915 residence—features glass-fronted cabinets and mahogany countertops. David hung the very traditional engravings in a most modern way. OPPOSITE: A view from the kitchen into the breakfast room. A reclaimed wide-board antique oak floor provides warmth and casualness.

ABOVE: In the first-floor family room, which also looks into the kitchen, we introduced a "Gothick" cornice molding, and David laid a Moroccan rug over a woven jute carpet. OPPOSITE: The breakfast room's ceiling is constructed from antique beams and planks; the walls are clad in lime-washed pecky cypress.

ABOVE AND OPPOSITE: The mudroom connects the breakfast room to the garage. Each of the family's children has a locker, while coat closets opposite them are louvered to keep the adults' coats and boots aired out. The wide antique oak floorboards are surrounded with a limestone border of the sort found in eighteenth-century Swedish houses. The peaked skylight makes the narrow space feel bigger and is a quick way to get a foolproof weather report.

completely cut off from its surroundings, and this enabled us to reconnect it to a beautiful new garden by Nashville landscape architect Gavin Duke. The resulting porosity is at once surprising and delightful: Boxwood is all about the pleasure of unconstrained seeing—from room to room, and from house to garden. Indeed, when my clients have a party, the main floor and the gardens that surround it become a vast social space through which their guests can circulate—a very modern experience in a historic setting.

Apart from my prior work with the family, I had another, more personal connection to Boxwood, one that strongly influenced its aesthetic direction: my admiration for the great American classicist Charles A. Platt (1861–1933). As an architecture student at Yale, I made a pilgrimage to Cornish, New Hampshire, to study the architect's own country house; then as now, I loved the understatement, the elegance, the proportions of his designs, his use of natural light, and his understanding of gardens (indeed, Platt began as a landscape painter and designer). In particular, his approach to detail influenced my thinking about the language of classicism; I immersed myself in a study of the architect's moldings and details prior to restoring the house, so as to become a more fluent speaker of "Platt."

Precisely understanding the subdued refinement of the original remained especially important because we planned to retain certain of the 1950s-era alterations and also to make some of our own. Many architects (and, for that matter, preservationists) believe that changes to a historic structure should broadcast their modernity, so as to establish a clear difference between old and new. I often disagree with this strategy, which is why, as we brought Boxwood back to what it had been, we made certain that any departures from its original plan and architectural character were nevertheless perfectly in tune with it.

The house's details, for example. My clients and I proposed to take Boxwood up a notch and make it a bit more like some of the grander residences for which Platt became famous—but not so much that its unpretentious modesty got lost. (Platt himself was a master at walking that line, as his pairing of an incredible Georgian front door with a simple shingled box demonstrates.) Toward this end, we introduced molding profiles, door surrounds, columns, pilasters, and other such elements based on Platt's own designs and keyed them to the function of the rooms: important spaces got more elaborate moldings, less significant ones received a simpler version of the language. Creating a hierarchy of detail was something Platt did well, and it guided us in remaining true to the house's spirit.

I had wanted to remove the entry portico, the centerpiece of the fifties renovation, but my clients loved it—as did many people in Nashville—for the memories it inspired. (Plus it's great when it rains.) So we decided that, if the portico had to stay, it should be re-proportioned and re-detailed to more closely resemble one that Platt himself might have designed. We tore off the existing one, replacing it with a tympanum pierced by an oculus window and with a thicker entablature, all supported by Doric (rather than Corinthian) columns. Speaking the classical language more precisely enabled us to integrate an element that previously had felt clumsy and extraneous.

While this is a story about architecture, it would be incomplete if I did not talk about the central role played by Boxwood's interior designer, David Netto. To be sure, the house required the sort of architectural rigor and discipline my office brought to it. But I'd be the first to admit that members of my profession (myself included) can sometimes carry a disciplined approach to an extreme. Decorators, on the other hand, are much more comfortable making seemingly arbitrary, counterintuitive associations, which is a good thing—sometimes you just need to loosen up. That's why I so enjoyed our collaboration with David: if we resolved Boxwood's programmatic issues and restored the authority of its classical bones, he invested it with a young, chic spirit entirely appropriate to our clients.

Often this was accomplished with an intriguing reversal of expectation. For the stone floor in the entry, for example, he took a very correct, classic shaded-block pattern and enlarged the scale, making it feel more abstract and modern. In a similar vein, I proposed a traditional wood-paneled library, but David wanted it to be different from the one you might find in such a correct, classical

house. He was a great admirer of a cabinet, designed by the French modernist Jean-Michel Frank in the 1930s, made of hand-gouged oak and suggested we treat the library that same way—as though it were a room-size piece of Art Deco furniture. The resulting interplay between the classical and modern sensibilities is at once very beautiful and entirely unexpected. David and I didn't always agree: I doubted, at first, his choice of a cola-colored lacquer for the loggia walls, and he initially objected to my insistence on painting the exterior brick a soft chalky white to make the house more Southern in flavor. But we each took a leap of faith and were both pleasantly surprised. Any residential architect who resists collaborating with an inspired decorator will do his project a great disservice.

My work on Boxwood proved to be among the most satisfying of my professional life. It offered a once-in-a-lifetime chance to work on a Platt residence and for clients who in-spired, challenged, and trusted us. In the end I am perhaps most happy with the balance of elegant formality and family comfort that we managed to achieve and the sense of interconnectedness that permeates the architecture and landscape holistically. Ultimately, we made many changes, and in fact took the building apart completely except for three of the four exterior walls. Even so, we didn't steal Boxwood's soul but rather resuscitated it—and in the process made a true and livable home that will nurture a family for many years to come.

ABOVE: A circa 1915 photograph of the rear of the original house. FOLLOWING PAGES: The restored garden façade, with a new limestone terrace stretching the full length of the house, overlooks Gavin Duke's new garden.

ABOVE: A terrace off the loggia at the western end of the house provides another point of connection to the grounds. OPPOSITE: Our new pergola overlooks the pool and frames multiple garden views.

# GATEWOOD
## BRINGING NEW LIFE TO A HISTORIC HOME

Architecturally speaking, there is a difference between renovation and restoration—one that becomes especially acute when the aim is to preserve the essence of a historic house. At Boxwood, we took great pains to bring back the spirit of Charles Platt's original design, and I think we succeeded. Yet without question, the house changed substantially: rooms were added and subtracted, spatial relationships reconfigured, walls demolished, details introduced that drew on Platt's vocabulary but had not initially been present. Our work may have captured the architect's sensibility, but it represented a renovation: an interweaving of old and new planning and programming in the service of both historic and contemporary imperatives.

When I am asked to work on an old residence, this is the more typical approach. People cherish the architecture of generations—or centuries—past. But they also want modern bathrooms, eat-in kitchens, and comfortable places to watch TV, and have no problem replanning their homes to make space for these things, as long as history is respected. And really, there would seem to be no other way—as the old saying goes, you can't make an omelet without breaking a few eggs.

Unless, as was the case with the William C. Gatewood house in Charleston, South Carolina, a magnificent Greek Revival residence completed in 1843, your clients request that you *restore* their home: that is, return it as faithfully as possible

to what it had been originally, as though it were a historic land-mark, while at the same time making the house as comfortably livable as the most newly minted, fully modernized of dwellings. What do you do when you're asked to make an omelet without breaking any eggs?

It was a challenge I actually embraced, as Gatewood turned out to be not only a singular antebellum mansion but also a fascinating, sometimes frustrating, architectural archaeology site. Richard "Moby" Marks, the Charleston restoration contractor who is this tale's true hero, describes the house's master, William Gatewood, as "a Bill Gates of his day"—a Virginia-born merchant who had made a fortune dealing in rice and cotton and chose to relocate to fashionable Charleston and build himself a home befitting his station. (The architect's name, intriguingly, is lost to history, but a local man named E. B. White oversaw Gatewood's construction, and some say it bears the distinctive stamp of his work.) The house is, in certain respects, very typical of its time: a classic Charleston "sideyard," so called for the stacked porches along the southern façade (known in local parlance as piazzas) overlooking an expanse of garden. It's a wonderfully unusual form, one that evolved, like many architectural typologies, in response to conditions: the piazzas shaded residents from the not infre-quently merciless Charleston sun, and the exposure caught the breezes floating in off the Ashley River to the southwest.

In other ways, however, Gatewood stood as a most un-usual, even modern, structure. First of all, there was the style—Greek Revival (or Regency, as it was known in Charleston) in the 1840s was considered the acme of leading-edge chic. The house's treatment of the vernacular also proved innovative. Originally, the piazzas of sideyards were exposed appendages to the solid mass of the house; you came in through a door at the piazza's street-facing end, walked down to the middle, and found the entrance and a stair hall on the cross axis. But concur-rent with the creation of Gatewood, the sideyard took an archi-tectural leap: the façade of the house was extended to cover the exposed piazza—to give the appearance of a single solid mass—and the entrance was relocated to the northern side of the fa-

çade, where an indoor main stairway balanced the open-air porches to the south. Thus Gatewood, upon completion, repre-sented at once a stylistic and typological sea change.

Gatewood's infrastructure was no less up-to-the-minute (for 1843). The house featured an underground drainage system around the perimeter that captured ground-level rainwater and channeled it out to the street, and the lead-lined roof also caught the rain, sending it into cisterns in the attic and basement as part of Gatewood's unusual indoor plumbing apparatus. Along with water, there was fire: the house also had gas lighting.

On a purely aesthetic level, the nearly 10,000-square-foot residence, four stories tall, forty-eight feet in width, and with eleven fireplaces, is astonishing—a *serious* house. Because of the grand scale of the rooms, there are relatively few of them; on the piano nobile, one effectively finds only three—communicating front and rear parlors, twenty feet square and with fourteen-foot-high ceilings, and an only slightly smaller dining parlor—all wrapped by the piazza. (These rooms also feature nine-foot-tall triple-hung windows that, with the lower sashes raised, provide full indoor-outdoor communication.) Above the ground-floor arcaded loggia, the porches unfold in the Doric order, with the second-floor columns on pedestals, the third story featuring fluted Doric columns that come down to the porch floor, and a parapet above. Details are exemplary, in particular the limestone-and-marble window surrounds on the street façade, and on the interior, carved moldings, ceiling medallions, and the S-shaped newel post—an amazing piece of mahogany sculpture—that greets you when you come through the front door.

Gatewood the man died in 1861; Gatewood the house was sold two years later, and it ultimately went through ten owners prior to my clients, undergoing numerous alterations

PREVIOUS PAGE: The exuberantly sculptural S-shaped mahogany newel post at the base of the main stair greets the visitor upon arrival at Gatewood House. OPPOSITE: The street façade immedi-ately following the restoration. The red mortar, close in color to the bricks, contributes to the house's sense of monumentality.

The Restoration
*of*
**The William C. Gatewood House**
Charleston, South Carolina

GRAPHIC  0  4  8  16  SCALE

along the way. The property originally had several outbuildings, notably a kitchen house just behind the main residence, in which all food preparation took place (a large pantry sat directly below the dining room); around the time of the Civil War, a small connecting structure was built to join the two, with a service stair just behind the dining room. Toward the rear of the grounds, there had been a substantial carriage house; it was sold off when the property was subdivided in the 1920s. And in a fall from gentility that would have intrigued Tennessee Williams, Gatewood served as a rooming house for several decades following World War II, with many of its small staircases and transitional zones cobbled into kitchens and bathrooms before

being reclaimed in the seventies as a single-family dwelling.

Despite the decades of battering, Gatewood became a kind of holy grail for my clients, a couple who'd been searching for an important historic house in the city for years (the husband's roots in Charleston go back ten generations). When they discovered and fell in love with Gatewood, it was not actually on the market—and so they simply kept on asking and asking (and getting repeatedly refused) until the owners gave in to their entreaties. As a restoration contractor with an intimate understanding of Charleston's architectural antiques, Moby Marks was the ideal man to return the house to its original glory. I came aboard, at first in a relatively modest capacity, to design a kitchen and sev-

SOUTH ELEVATION

THE RESTORATION
*of*
THE WILLIAM C. GATEWOOD HOUSE
CHARLESTON, SOUTH CAROLINA

0   4   8        16
GRAPHIC                    SCALE

eral bathrooms and to ensure that, as work progressed, any new elements maintained the house's classical pedigree.

If I served as the project's design eye, Moby turned out to be our private eye, an architectural sleuth capable of nosing out, from countless small clues, Gatewood's long-lost original form. But he had first to apply his talents to assessing the house's structural issues, and those, to everyone's surprise and dismay, proved to be titanic. I, for one, was completely fooled—when I first visited, I thought, *How beautiful, it just needs some paint.* In reality, beneath the splendid classical details, Gatewood was near to ruin. Moby's investigations revealed that the bricks along the south façade of the major parlors had delaminated from one another, to

the degree that the ceiling joists had detached from their connections to the walls. One of the kitchen house façades, we discovered, was leaning out some eight inches, and the situation on the main house's north side proved to be even more grave—the wall had pulled away, and the entire main stair sagged perilously into

OPPOSITE: Gatewood's grandeur and scale in comparison to the other houses with which it shares the street, strongly apparent in this elevation, was an innovation in 1843. ABOVE: The covered piazzas, seen in this elevation, are the signature element of the Charleston sideyard house. Also visible is the kitchen house at the property's rear, joined to the main house by a connecting structure—known in architectural parlance as a hyphen—added shortly after the Civil War.

the side alley. The cistern in the attic had leaked, rotting the trusses that held up the roof. Worst of all, Moby surmised that a rear corner of Gatewood had in all likelihood fallen down in the great Charleston earthquake of 1886 and been rebuilt very haphazardly, after which that entire part of the house had sunk a full seven inches. In truth, it was a kind of miracle that the whole place hadn't collapsed into a heap of bricks.

Moby had little choice: over four years, he took Gatewood almost entirely apart and completely reconstructed it. The tilting kitchen wall came down and went back up again plumb using all of the old bricks (Moby even concocted the original recipe for Gatewood's distinctive red mortar). Working with our amazing structural engineer, Craig Bennett, he reinforced the

dramatic three-story main stair with steel and used it, in effect, as a giant diagonal bracing beam, to which he securely bolted the north façade—indeed, Craig wove an enormous amount of steel invisibly into all of the house's bones. While the fireplace mantels were removed and the chimney walls rebuilt, Moby held the win-

PREVIOUS PAGES: Two views of the second-floor piazza. The grandeur of the house is evident in the marble surround of the window that opens into the piazza and in the stately, elegant colonnade. ABOVE: The covered loggia that forms the base of the three-story piazza, with a view back toward the rear garden. OPPOSITE: The raised pool, designed by Deborah Nevins, is deep enough for swimming. The pool steps are based on the stone blocks traditionally used to mount a horse; the granite coping along the pool's edge ingeniously cantilevers out over the boxwood hedge.

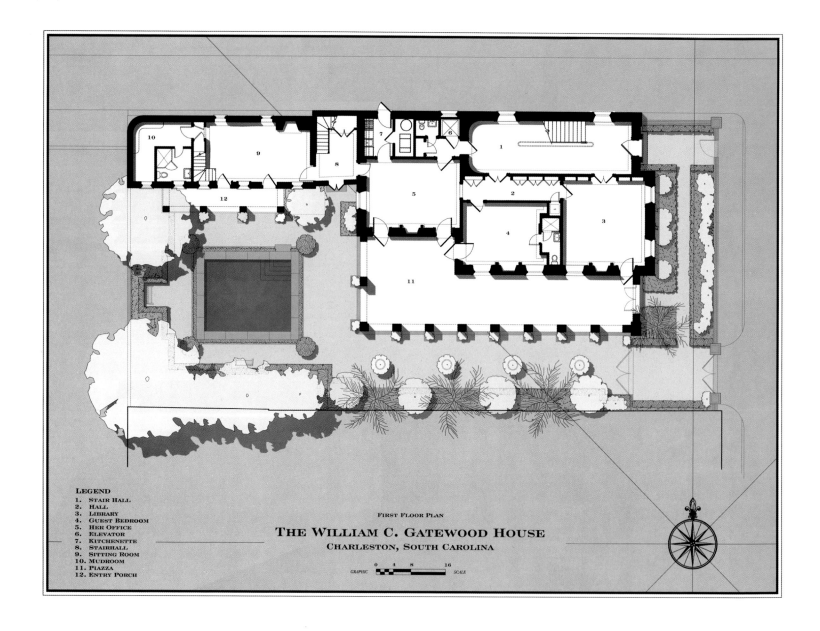

FIRST FLOOR PLAN

THE WILLIAM C. GATEWOOD HOUSE
CHARLESTON, SOUTH CAROLINA

GRAPHIC   0  4  8    16   SCALE

dow frames precisely in place, preserving the original glass, sashes, and architraves. Damaged details, among them the extraordinary carved-plaster ceiling medallions taken from one of Minard Lafever's influential nineteenth-century architectural pattern books, were reconstructed with equivalent care and fidelity.

As for Moby's sleuthing skills, he revealed a genius for pulling Sheetrock off the walls, studying the ghost marks on the original studs, and understanding what had been there when William Gatewood walked the halls. This was especially invaluable as so many interstitial spaces had been repurposed in the residence's boardinghouse years. When Moby demolished a third-floor bathroom, for example, he found suggestions of a former staircase, which we replaced, enabling us to reclaim proper possession of the house's fourth floor. He also discovered evidence suggesting that the kitchen house had once had its own porch, another lost feature that was put back. Watching Moby crack one "case" after another, I joked that Gatewood felt like a particularly gripping episode of *CSI: Charleston*.

At this point in the story, you might well be wondering what I was doing. If my presiding mantra is always to make tradition livable, on this job, it was proving to be a true braintwister given my strict-preservationist clients. The mandate was that everything original to the house in plan and detail must, if at all possible, remain. In other words, it was acceptable

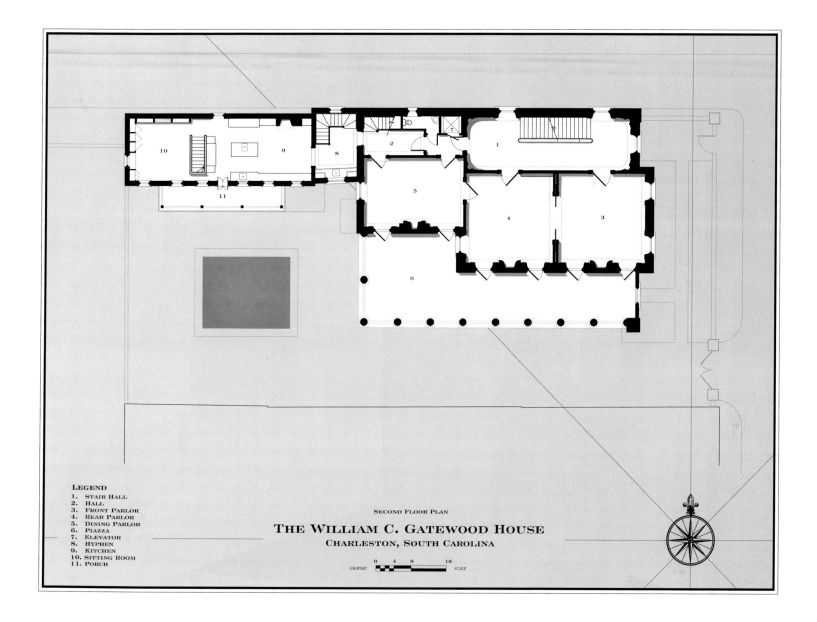

SECOND FLOOR PLAN

# THE WILLIAM C. GATEWOOD HOUSE
## CHARLESTON, SOUTH CAROLINA

GRAPHIC    0   4   8        16    SCALE

to have modern bathrooms as long as their design remained appropriate to the fundamental style of the residence. It was *not* acceptable, however, to tear down a historic wall to make those bathrooms the "right" size. When I first proposed to do so, my client shook her head. "You don't understand: we don't *do* that in Charleston. We respect the original," she explained. "It's perfectly respectable, in a historic house, to have a sink in one closet, a toilet in another, and a shower down the hall."

Needless to say, I was, at first, perplexed. Given that part of my job was to help my clients to be able to live at Gatewood in a modern way, this kind of solution seemed inconceivable. Yet I greatly respected their desire to honor and preserve

the sublime example of a very special, very specific moment in Charleston's history that was their home. And so the challenge (and, as it turned out, the fun) of the project derived from embedding all of the necessities of contemporary life in the residence without removing a single wall or original feature.

OPPOSITE: The plan of the restored residence showing the relationships between the house and garden and the principal and secondary structures. ABOVE: The second-floor plan reveals the grand scale of the three original parlors in front and the newly conceived kitchen/breakfast/family room in the kitchen house, both of which communicate easily with one another for an agreeable formal-informal mix that is so vital to a livable house today.

ABOVE AND OPPOSITE: The grand stair, rising up three stories through the house's formal wing, has a sinuous, sculptural quality. A period Charleston color called Rhett Pumpkin was selected by color consultant Eve Ashcraft to give these formal spaces a warm glow and lend a vibrant articulation to the architectural elements. Craig Bennett, Gatewood's restoration engineer, reinforced the stair with steel, enabling it now to serve as a beam to hold the exterior wall in place.

The house's double parlors feature original triple-hung sash windows that open directly onto the piazza and serve as de facto doors. The stone chimneypieces, also original, had to be dismantled and reinstalled over the course of construction. Original as well are the heart pine floors, carved wood door and window surrounds, and pocket doors (which still work).

ABOVE AND OPPOSITE: A scenic mural with trompe l'oeil wainscoting below was created for Gatewood's dining parlor by de Gournay; its sepia tone brings warmth to the room, making it a magical setting for meals. Gatewood's broad doorways connect the parlors visually as well as actually and underscore the house's natural flow.

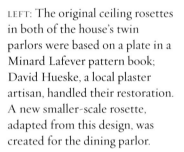

LEFT: The original ceiling rosettes in both of the house's twin parlors were based on a plate in a Minard Lafever pattern book; David Hueske, a local plaster artisan, handled their restoration. A new smaller-scale rosette, adapted from this design, was created for the dining parlor.

That meant many things. Tucking a tiny powder room underneath the stair on the second floor. Inserting an elevator into what had once been a closet. Installing a very long tub deck in the third-floor master bath so that the stairway rising just beneath it could maintain the proper headroom (the slanted back of the tub matches the stair slope perfectly). Slipping a small bath into a former dressing room. Weaving in new electrical systems, central air-conditioning, and Internet lines. But what I enjoyed the most were opportunities for what might be described as architectural sleight of hand. One of my favorites can be found in the bath that adjoins the ground-floor guest bedroom. There was only a three-foot-wide slot of closet space into which we had to fit a shower, sink, and toilet. That really isn't possible. So we created what appears to be a small nineteenth-century wardrobe cabinet in the guest bedroom, which

is in fact a hollow space we used to slip in all of the bathroom's necessities. By disguising our extension of the bath into the adjoining room as a closet, we were able to maintain the original plan—and if a future owner wants to preserve it more precisely, our intervention can be easily extracted.

An essential component of making historic homes livable in a contemporary way involves creating strong, fluent connections between their formal and informal parts—vertically as well as horizontally. Toward that end, we put back all of the stairways that had been removed over the years: the small service stair outside the dining parlor; another that connects the new second-floor butler's pantry to the ground; and a spiral one that links the third floor to the attic. The most dramatic horizontal change followed our decision to move the kitchen from the bottom to the second floor of the kitchen house and—by creating doorways on either side of the connecting structure—open it up completely to Gatewood's more formal living and dining spaces. Strengthening that connection helped minimize the divide between serving and served areas typically found in older residences.

Indeed, it would be hard to overstate how important the vernacular character of the kitchen house is to the success of the overall design, as it serves as an essential counterbalance to the near-palatial grandeur of Gatewood's public rooms. The new second-floor kitchen we styled as a classic twenty-first-century multiuse space, with a table and chairs for casual dining, a cooking zone that's big enough for the whole family to participate if they so choose, and a den area with dog-friendly sofas and a flat-screen TV; on the ground floor, we created a big sitting room with an antique brick floor that opens up through two doors to the garden—ideal for both hanging out in the hot months and setting up catering for large parties. As a result, the kitchen and main houses coexist on a more equal footing; you never feel like you can't take a break from Gatewood's grandeur. And because the two structures communicate with one another through those strong horizontal connections, the family can move with ease and comfort between the two worlds. (Another contributor to Gatewood's informal side is the main house's ground floor: with a bedroom, sitting room, kitchenette, and bath, all of which can be closed off from the upper floors and function independently—it serves as a freestanding apartment for visiting friends and relatives.)

Because the couple proposed to gradually build a furniture collection appropriate to Gatewood's period—conceivably the work of a lifetime—we knew there wouldn't be a lot of decoration in the house at first. Instead, I brought in the color consultant Eve Ashcraft, a frequent collaborator with whom I first worked on my own home, to help develop a "color story" that would foreground the design details, enhance the architecture's volumetric qualities, and also speak to Gatewood's roots. The apogee of this effort, I believe, can be seen in the rich salmon color of the stair halls, a historic Charleston shade known as "Rhett Pumpkin."

Landscape designer Deborah Nevins, another frequent collaborator, provided Gatewood with one of its most unusual—and purely delightful—elements. When my clients purchased the house, they inherited what may well have been the first outdoor swimming pool installed at a Charleston sideyard house. Unfortunately, it ate up the entire garden, was surrounded by concrete, and had to go. But my clients did still want a place to cool off, and they liked the idea of developing something original; they believed, quite rightly, that this was the one place where no verifiable historical record existed, and wished to make their own contribution to Gatewood's aesthetic history.

I have always admired Deborah's inventiveness and restraint; one of her great strengths lies in knowing exactly how much is just enough. Here at Gatewood, her nearly square swimming pool has the serene appearance of a garden reflecting pool, raised eighteen inches above the ground (it is, of course, much deeper) and with granite coping stones that cantilever over a low boxwood hedge; you step up to the pool on blocks very similar to those used historically in Charleston to mount a horse. It is absolutely beautiful, as is the way you approach the back garden from the street: Deborah laid a bed of crushed oyster shells on what had once been a driveway and atop it set an allée of Meyer lemon trees in enormous terra-cotta pots. The welcoming crunch of the shells beneath one's shoes and the trees' fragrance remind us that a great garden isn't only a feast for the eyes.

The resurrection of the Gatewood house reinforced three of the most useful lessons I've learned over more than twenty years of practice. One is the incalculable value of collaboration: Eve, Deborah, Craig, Moby, and of course our incredible clients all contributed to the outcome. Another lesson is the need to immerse oneself—with humility—in the classical language of a project and learn to speak it well enough so that the success of one's work is measured, ironically, by the degree to which it remains undetectable. Above all, my experience at Gatewood reminded me that residential architecture—whether the project is new or old—is about more than designing a molding. It is about understanding your client's desires and figuring out how they can be translated into a home that answers them in every way: functionally, comfortably, and with elegance. Doing so successfully is one of the most enduring satisfactions of an architect's life and something I strive for every day in my work.

ABOVE: One of the few rooms in the house to receive full decoration, the light and airy master bedroom features a traditional Southern four-poster bed purchased for the room.
OPPOSITE: One of Gatewood's many new bathrooms we inserted into former rooms, this one the new master bath. We added the interior window to bring light into the stair hall beyond.
FOLLOWING PAGE: Details of contemporary living were adapted to adhere to the owners' insistence on authenticity (the wardrobe at upper left and right was created to contain a new bathroom).

PREVIOUS PAGE: A new stairway reconnects the fourth floor to the rest of the house.
ABOVE AND OPPOSITE: The fourth-floor bathroom, newly created for the house,
preserves the original plaster walls, unfinished pine floors, and painted woodwork;
its simplicity is in keeping with Gatewood's architectural hierarchies.

The ground floor of the restored kitchen house. While the stair is original, the new floor was constructed from antique bricks and follows historic precedent. The gentle color palette, also faithful to Gatewood's period, showcases Eve Ashcraft's sensitivity to time and place. The relaxed vernacular character of the kitchen house stands in notable contrast to the main house's intense formality— low versus high classicism.

245

ABOVE: A view across the connecting structure from the main house into the kitchen-house wing reveals the new stair created to link the second floor to the garden. OPPOSITE: The new second-floor pantry we built in the connecting structure conceals modern appliances within the cabinetry. We preserved the original brick wall of the kitchen house.

ABOVE AND OPPOSITE: This room, on the second floor of the kitchen house, speaks to contemporary needs and a twenty-first-century way of life: it incorporates a sitting area with a television, an open kitchen, and a breakfast table (in front of the room's original fireplace) and, not surprisingly, is one of Gatewood's most popular spaces during parties.

LEFT: The old swimming pool, one of the first to be installed in a Charleston sideyard house, robbed the garden of its charm and, indeed, of the presence of nature. ABOVE: Deborah Nevins's artful reimagination of the pool left ample room for landscape. The porch on the kitchen house was reconstructed once a foundation, discovered beneath the concrete, revealed its prior existence. OPPOSITE: Deborah's allée of Meyer lemon trees, planted in grandly scaled terra-cotta pots, sits atop a path paved with crushed oyster shells and draws the visitor back to the rear garden.

# RESOURCES

## DOOR, WINDOW, AND CABINET HARDWARE

Ball and Ball Hardware Reproductions
*(brass and wrought iron)*
www.ballandball.com

E. R. Butler & Co.
*(brass, nickel, bronze, and silver)*
www.erbutler.com

Frank Allart & Company
*(brass and nickel)*
www.allart.co.uk

Historic Housefitters Co.
*(hand-forged wrought iron)*
www.historichousefitters.com

Katonah Architectural Hardware
*(brass, nickel, and bronze)*
www.katonahhardware.com

Sun Valley Bronze
*(forged bronze)*
www.sunvalleybronze.com

## PLUMBING FIXTURES, FITTINGS, AND BATH ACCESSORIES

Kallista
www.kallista.com

Newport Brass
www.newportbrass.com

Samuel Heath
www.samuel-heath.com

Barber Wilsons & Co. Ltd.
www.barwil.co.uk

Urban Archaeology
www.urbanarchaeology.com

Waterworks
www.waterworks.com

## ANTIQUE WOOD FLOORS

Baba Wood
www.baba.com

The Hudson Co. Vintage
Wood and Stone
www.hudson-co.com

## STONE AND TILE

Ann Sacks Tile & Stone
www.annsacks.com

Exquisite Surfaces
www.xsurfaces.com

Nemo Tile Company, Inc.
www.nemotile.com

Paris Ceramics
www.parisceramics.com

Stone Source
www.stonesource.com

Waterworks
www.waterworks.com

## DECORATIVE LIGHTING– EXTERIOR

Ann Morris Antiques
www.annmorrisantiques.com

Charles Edwards Antiques
www.charlesedwards.com

Howe's Designs
www.howelondon.com

Period Lighting Fixtures
www.periodlighting.com

Treillage, Ltd.
www.bunnywilliams.com/treillage

Urban Archaeology
www.urbanarchaeology.com

Vaughan Designs
www.vaughandesigns.com

## DECORATIVE LIGHTING– INTERIOR

Ann Morris Antiques
www.annmorrisantiques.com

Charles Edwards Antiques
www.charlesedwards.com

Restoration Hardware
www.restorationhardware.com

Robert Kime
www.robertkime.com

Soane
www.soane.co.uk

Urban Archaeology
www.urbanarchaeology.com

Vaughan Designs
www.vaughandesigns.com

Visual Comfort
www.circalighting.com

Waterworks
www.waterworks.com

## ANTIQUE AND REPRODUCTION MANTELS

A. & R. Asta Limited
(antique wood and stone)
www.astafireplaces.com

Barry H. Perry
(antique and reproduction stone)
www.barryhperry.com

Chesney's
(antique and reproduction stone)
www.chesneys.com

Jamb Limited
(antique and reproduction stone)
www.jamblimited.com

Francis J. Purcell Antiques
(antique American wood)
www.francisjpurcell.com

## DECORATIVE PLASTER AND SCAGLIOLA

Balmer Architectural Mouldings, Inc.
(plaster moldings and columns)
www.balmer.com

David Flaharty, sculptor
(plaster ceiling medallions)
215-234-8242

David B. Hueske
(restoration)
843-693-9405

Sulieman Studios
(scagliola and custom plaster elements)
215-348-5707

## CUSTOM FURNITURE AND SPECIALTY MILLWORK

Atelier Viollet
www.atelierviollet.com

Laszlo S. Inc.
www.laszlo.biz

Thomas W. Newman, cabinetmaker
www.thomaswnewman.com

## DECORATIVE METALWORK AND FINISHING

Empire Metal Finishing
www.empiremetal.net

Les Métalliers Champenois
www.l-m-c.com

## REPRODUCTION ANTIQUE MIRROR AND GLASS

S. A. Bendheim, Ltd.
www.bendheim.com

Hines Studios
www.hinesstudios.net

## DECORATIVE PAINTING

Jean Carrau Interieurs
www.jeancarrau.com

John Weidl Associates, Inc.
917-636-5067

## SCENIC AND BLOCK-PRINTED WALLPAPER

Adelphi Paper Hangings
www.adelphipaperhangings.com

De Gournay Ltd.
www.degournay.com

George Spencer Designs
www.georgespencer.com

## GARDEN FURNITURE

Hervé Baume Antiques &
   Garden Furniture
www.herve-baume.com

Janus et Cie
www.janusetcie.com

McKinnon and Harris
www.mckinnonharris.com

Munder-Skiles
www.munder-skiles.com

Treillage, Ltd.
www.bunnywilliams.com/treillage

# ACKNOWLEDGMENTS

The Saint-Exupéry passage that opens this book was sent to me not too long ago by my mother—just another example of those random missives a parent shares with a child hoping that it will inspire (it did!). In truth, both of my parents, along with my stepmother Robin and my four grandparents, have been tremendous inspirations to me over the years, and their particular contributions to shaping my sensibility as an architect—and as a person—I must acknowledge first. Equally so, the deep bond I have with my three siblings has been such a steady and important part of my life—both a sail in a good wind and a sheltering harbor in a storm. After all, family, more than architecture, is the true foundation of home.

I think that most people know that design is a collaborative art, and thus the success of a practice depends on relationships. There may be one person on a project who has a guiding vision or idea, but it is the collaborations we have, often with a myriad of people, that inevitably contribute to making the final product sing. That is absolutely true with my practice, starting with the incredibly talented group of people in my office with whom I have had the privilege to work during the last ten years. These include Michael J. Benson Jr., Laura S. Blochwitz, Aimee P. Buccellato, Kevin M. Buccellato, Alejandra Cesar, Maria Cruz, Micah Dawson, Sheila Delaney, Brad Devendorf, George Distefano, Whitley Esteban, Tessa Fleck, Sarah Fout, Michael Harris, Katrina E. Hendricks, Benjamin Hoyumpa, Catherine L. Kirchhoff, Whitney Kirk, Teresa M. Lopes, Monica Luca, Ian Manire, Nick Markovich, Brendan P. McNee, Michael Mesko, Teresa R. Michailovs, Ellen K. Mitchell, Tony Moniaga, Molua Muldown, Stefanie A. Mustian, Khara Nemitz, Lenore Passavanti, Mark E. Pledger, Darin Quan, Jahlay Rae, Danielle Y. Reed, Diana T. Reising, Manuel Tan, Chris S. Taylor, Louis P. Taylor, Jean-Marie Truchard, Christine Valiquette, Joseph P. Vega, Riccardo Vicenzino, Laura Welsh, and Matthew Winter.

I have been equally blessed by the many wonderful collaborations I have had outside the office as well—with talented colleagues who have inspired, challenged, and mentored me in my work and, best of all, many of whom have become good friends too. They include Marc Appleton, Eve Ashcraft, Linda Atkins, Bill Brockschmidt, Robert and Jacob Bump, Rhett Butler, Richard Cameron, Drew Casertano, Courtney Coleman, Joe Coppo, John Cottrell, Valerie Christou, Stela and Radu Danau, Richard Dragisic, Gavin Duke, Keith Granet, Victoria Hagan, Tom Maciag, Tom Marble, Lindsay McCrum, May Nakib, Nasser Nakib, David Netto, Deborah Nevins, Ben Page, Miles Redd, John Rosselli, Laszlo Sallay, Tom Savage, Alan Siegel, Michael Smith, Niall Smith, Ahmad Sulieman, Bob Stern, Dan Taylor, Daniela Voith, Jean Wiart, Angus Wilkie, and Bunny Williams, for whose lovely foreword to this book—not to mention her long friendship—I am also deeply grateful. These relationships have enriched my work immeasurably and in many cases deepened my understanding of what it means to design and build well. I owe a great debt to each of them.

I must also thank Mark Ferguson, John Murray, Oscar Shamamian, and Donald Rattner, whose mentorship for nearly a decade while I worked in their office—in its various incarnations—turned my intuitive, youthful enthusiasm for traditional houses and gardens into an advanced education in classicism as well as in architecture, both as an art *and* as a profession. I learned so much from each of them and am enormously grateful for that. I am also indebted to them for my introduction to the Institute of Classical Architecture & Art, which has in turn become my great passion for the last twenty years.

To the many receptive and encouraging magazine editors who have supported me in my work over the years and the talented photographers who enriched the efforts of my firm and brought them so stunningly to life, I am also profoundly grateful.

Of course, without great patrons, there wouldn't be any great architecture, to photograph or to publish—to paraphrase the English classicist Edwin Lutyens. As architects of houses, we undertake a kind of miraculous transaction with our clients: they share with us their dreams and aspirations—and the financial means to realize them—challenging, inspiring, and trusting us along the way; and in return, we give back to them something tangible out of our imagination, and with it a part of ourselves. We give to them what "home" means to us, and it is a privilege that is both humbling and exhilarating. I am profoundly appreciative, every day, of having this opportunity to partner with them.

If a book is a way to take stock of all this work, it is thus also a formidable challenge. I must thank Charles Miers at Rizzoli for giving me this extraordinary opportunity and for guiding me through it; Kathleen Jayes, my brilliant editor, for her discerning eye and flawless good judgment; and my amazing creative partners in the project: Marc Kristal, my erudite, funny, and laconic cowriter; Chris Gray, my gifted wizard of images; Doug Turshen and Steve Turner, my infinitely imaginative and unflappable book designers; and last but certainly not least, Jill Cohen for her taste, good humor, encouragement, and unwavering honesty, which helped me find the book I had in me.

Finally, I must thank Amalia Lora, Dolores Vega, Keelie Christman, Clive Lodge, Diana Herold, and Richard, Christopher, and Phillip Carroll for all they have done over the years to make the places I have called home such a joy.

# PHOTOGRAPHY CREDITS

Christopher Baker: Pages 87, 227, 235, 238, 251

Max Kim-Bee: Pages 58, 59, 183, 187, 197, 198-199

Fernando Bengoechea: Pages 5, 66, 67, 100-101, 112, 116-117, 119, 120, 121, 123, 125

Carter Berg: Pages 14, 25, 31, 32 (upper right), 36 (upper right), 40-41, 42 (upper right), 43 (upper left), 46, 54, 55, 60-61, 68, 69, 74, 78-79, 92-93, 136-137, 146, 147, 166, 167

Henry Bourne: Page 45

Paul Costello: Pages 17, 22, 23, 28, 29, 32 (lower left, bottom right), 33, 34, 35, 36 (upper left, lower left), 38, 39, 42 (lower right), 43 (upper right), 47, 49, 50-51, 52-53, 59, 70, 71, 148, 149, 150, 151, 152, 153, 154, 155, 156, 157, 158, 159, 160, 161, 162, 163, 164, 165, 219, 221, 224, 225, 230, 231, 232-233, 234, 236, 239, 240 (upper left, upper right, lower left, lower right), 241, 242, 243, 244-245, 246, 247, 248, 249

Don Freeman: Page 44

Dana Gallagher: Page 73

John M. Hall: Pages 57, 103, 110, 114-115, 130, 255

Erik KVALSVIK: Page 113

© Eric Roth: Pages 27, 26, 36 (lower right), 43 (bottom right)

Gil Schafer III: Pages 2-3, 5, 12-13, 176, 213 (author's collection), 26, 75, 81, 82, 83, 84, 85, 86 (upper right, lower left, lower right), 98, 99, 102, 105, 106 (upper left, upper right, lower left, lower right), 107, 109, 126, 131, 177, 226, 250 (upper, bottom)

© René and Barbara Stoeltie: Pages 63, 64, 65

Fritz von der Schulenburg/ The Interior Archive: Pages 9, 62, 111, 118, 122, 127

William Waldron: Page 21

Jonathan Wallen: Pages 6, 20, 32 (upper left), 37, 42 (upper left and lower left), 43 (lower left), 76-77, 86 (upper left), 88-89, 90, 91, 94, 97, 128-129, 133, 138, 140 (upper, lower), 141, 143, 144-145, 168, 169, 170, 171, 172-173, 175, 178-179, 182, 184-185, 186-188, 189, 190-191, 192-193, 195, 196, 200, 201, 202, 203, 204, 205, 206, 207, 208, 209, 210, 211, 214-215, 216, 217

Drawings by G. P. Schafer Architect, PLLC: Pages 19, 104, 135, 180, 181, 222, 223, 228, 229

Maxfield Parrish Image, Page 11, used by permission: Art © Maxfield Parrish Family, LLC/Licensed by VAGA, New York, NY

First published in the United States of America in 2012
by Rizzoli International Publications, Inc.
300 Park Avenue South
New York, NY 10010
www.rizzoliusa.com

© 2011 Gil Schafer III

2013 2014 2015 / 10 9 8 7 6 5

Distributed in the U.S. trade by Random House, New York

Designed by Doug Turshen with Steve Turner

Printed in China

ISBN-13: 978-0-8478-3872-1

Library of Congress Catalog Control Number: 2012934112